A Treasury of
SHORTER VERSE

Wishes

Go, little book, and wish to all
Flowers in the garden, meat in the hall,
A bin of wine, a spice of wit,
A house with lawns enclosing it,
A living river by the door,
A nightingale in the sycamore.

ROBERT LOUIS STEVENSON (1850–94)

A Treasury of
SHORTER VERSE

BLUE HERON BOOKS

Vancouver

First published in Canada in 2004 by
Blue Heron Books, 9050 Shaughnessy Street
Vancouver, B.C. V6P 6E5
(604) 323-7100
www.raincoast.com

ISBN 1 897035 05 5

Text © Book Blocks 2003

Editorial selection by Rosemary Gray
Typeset in Great Britain by Antony Gray
Printed and bound in China

Contents

(The title of each section is taken from the first poem in that section)

Trailing Clouds of Glory

Our Birth is but a Sleep

Our birth is but a sleep and a forgetting:
The soul that rises with us, our life's star,
  Hath had elsewhere its setting,
   And cometh from afar:
   Not in entire forgetfulness,
   And not in utter nakedness,
But trailing clouds of glory do we come
   From God, who is our home:
Heaven lies about us in our infancy!
Shades of the prison-house begin to close
   Upon the growing boy
    But he beholds the light, and
     whence it flows,

He sees it in his joy;
The youth, who daily farther from the east
　　Must travel, still is nature's priest,
　　And by the vision splendid
　　Is on his way attended;
At length the man perceives it die away,
And fade into the light of common day.

WILLIAM WORDSWORTH (1770–1850)
from *Intimations of Immortality*

Infant Sorrow

My mother groaned, my father wept;
Into the dangerous world I leapt;
Helpless, naked, piping loud,
Like a fiend hid in a cloud.

Struggling in my father's hands,
Striving against my swaddling-bands,

Bound and weary, I thought best
To sulk upon my mother's breast.

WILLIAM BLAKE (1757–1827)

Sephestia's Song to her Child

Weep not my wanton smile upon my knee:
When thou art old there's grief enough for thee.
   Mother's wag, pretty boy,
   Father's sorrow, father's joy.
   When thy father first did see
   Such a boy by him and me,
   He was glad, I was woe,
   Fortune changed made him so,
   When he left his pretty boy,
   Last his sorrow, first his joy.
Weep not my wanton smile upon my knee:
When thou art old there's grief enough for thee.
   Streaming tears that never stint,

Like pearl drops from a flint,
Fell by course from his eyes,
That one another's place supplies:
Thus he griev'd in every part,
Tears of blood fell from his heart,
When he left his pretty boy,
Father's sorrow, father's joy.
Weep not my wanton smile upon my knee:
When thou art old there's grief enough for thee.
The wanton smiled, father wept:
Mother cried, baby leapt:
More he crowed, more we cried;
Nature could not sorrow hide.
He must go, he must kiss
Child and mother, baby bliss:
For he left his pretty boy,
Father's sorrow, father's joy.
Weep not my wanton smile upon my knee:
When thou art old there's grief enough for thee.

ROBERT GREENE (1560–92)

Infant Joy

'I have no name:
I am but two days old.'
What shall I call thee?
'I happy am,
Joy is my name.'
Sweet joy befall thee!

Pretty Joy!
Sweet Joy, but two days old.
Sweet Joy I call thee
Thou dost smile,
I sing the while,
Sweet joy befall thee!

WILLIAM BLAKE (1757–1827)

De Puero Balbutiente

Methinks 'tis pretty sport to hear a child,
Rocking a word in mouth yet undefiled;
The tender racquet rudely plays the sound,
Which, weakly bandied, cannot back rebound;
And the soft air the softer roof doth kiss,
With a sweet dying and a pretty miss,
Which hears no answer yet from the white rank
Of teeth, not risen from their coral bank.
The alphabet is searched for letters soft,
To try a word before it can be wrought,
And when it slideth forth, it goes as nice
As when a man does walk upon the ice.

THOMAS BASTARD (1566–1618)

A Little Child, a Limber Elf

A little child, a limber elf,
Singing, dancing to itself,
A fairy thing with red round cheeks,
That always finds, and never seeks,
Makes such a vision to the sight
As fills a father's eyes with light;
And pleasures flow in so thick and fast
Upon his heart, that he at last
Must needs express his love's excess
With words of unmeant bitterness.
Perhaps 'tis pretty to force together
Thoughts so all unlike each other;
To mutter and mock a broken charm,
To dally with wrong that does no harm.
Perhaps 'tis tender too and pretty
At each wild word to feel within
A sweet recoil of love and pity.
And what, if in a world of sin

(O sorrow and shame should this be true!)
Such giddiness of heart and brain
Comes seldom save from rage and pain,
So talks as it's most used to do.

SAMUEL TAYLOR COLERIDGE (1772–1834)

A Parental Ode to My Son, aged three years and five months

Thou happy, happy elf!
(But stop – first let me kiss away that tear)
    Thou tiny image of myself
(My love, he's poking peas into his ear!)
    Thou merry, laughing sprite,
    With spirits feather-light,
Untouched by sorrow and unsoil'd by sin –
(Good heavens, the child is swallowing a pin!)

Thou little tricksy Puck!
With antic toys so funnily bestuck,
Light as the singing bird that wings the air –
(The door! The door! he'll tumble down the stair!)
　　Thou darling of thy sire!
(Why, Jane, he'll set his pinafore afire!)
　　Thou imp of mirth and joy!
In love's dear chain so bright and strong a link,
Thou idol of thy parents – (Drat the boy!
　　There goes my ink!)

　　Thou cherub – but of earth
Fit playfellow for Fays, by moonlight pale,
　　In harmless sport and mirth
(That dog will bite him if he pulls its tail!)
Thou human humming bee, extracting honey
From every blossom in the world that blows,
　Singing in Youth's Elysium ever sunny –
(Another tumble! – That's his precious nose!)

　　Thy father's pride and hope!
(He'll break the mirror with that skipping rope!)

With pure heart newly stamped from Nature's mint –
    (Where *did* he learn that squint?)
    Thou young, domestic dove!
(He'll have that jug off, with another shove!)
  Dear nursling of the hymeneal nest!
  (Are those torn clothes his best?)
     Little epitome of man!
(He'll climb upon the table; that's his plan!)
Touch'd with the beauteous tints of dawning life –
    (He's got a knife!)

    Thou enviable being,
No storms, no clouds, in thy blue sky foreseeing,
    Play on, play on,
    My elfin John!
Toss the light ball – bestride the stick –
(I knew so many cakes would make him sick!)
With fancies buoyant as the thistledown,
Prompting the face grotesque, and antic brisk,
    With many a lamb-like frisk –
(He's got the scissors, snipping at your gown!)

Thou pretty, opening rose!
(Go to your mother, child, and wipe your nose!)
Balmy, and breathing music like the South
(He really brings my heart into my mouth!)
Fresh as the morning, brilliant as its star –
(I wish that window had an iron bar!)
Bold as the hawk, yet gentle as the dove –
    (I'll tell you what, my love,
I cannot write unless he's sent above!)

THOMAS HOOD (1799–1845)

Rhyme for a Child Viewing a Naked Venus in a Painting of the Judgement of Paris

He gazed and gazed and gazed and gazed,
Amazed, amazed, amazed, amazed.

ROBERT BROWNING (1812–89)

A Letter to the Honourable Lady Miss Margaret Cavendish-Holles-Harley

My noble, lovely, little Peggy,
Let this, my first epistle, beg ye,
At dawn of morn, and close of even,
To lift your heart and hands to heaven:
In double beauty say your pray'r,
Our father first, then *notre père*;
And, dearest child, along the day,
In ev'rything you do and say,
Obey and please my lord and lady,
So God shall love, and angels aid, ye.

If to these precepts you attend,
No second letter need I send,
And so I rest your constant friend,

M.P.

MATTHEW PRIOR (1664–1749)

18

The Toys

My little son, who looked from thoughtful eyes
And moved and spoke in quiet grown-up wise,
Having my law the seventh time disobeyed,
I struck him, and dismissed
With hard words and unkissed –
His Mother, who was patient, being dead.
Then, fearing lest his grief should hinder sleep,
I visited his bed,
But found him slumbering deep,
With darkened eyelids, and their lashes yet
From his late sobbing wet.
And I, with moan,
Kissing away his tears, left others of my own;
For, on a table drawn beside his head,
He had put, within his reach,
A box of counters and a red-veined stone,
A piece of glass abraded by the beach,
And six or seven shells,

A bottle with bluebells
And two French copper coins, ranged there
                              with careful art,
To comfort his sad heart.
So when that night I prayed
To God, I wept, and said:
'Ah, when at last we lie with trancèd breath,
Not vexing Thee in death,
And Thou rememberest of what toys
We made our joys,
How weakly understood
Thy great commanded good,
Then, fatherly not less
Than I whom Thou hast moulded from the clay,
Thou'lt leave Thy wrath, and say,
"I will be sorry for their childishness." '

COVENTRY PATMORE (1823–96)

I Remember, I Remember

I remember, I remember
The house where I was born,
The little window where the sun
Came peeping in at morn;
He never came a wink too soon,
Nor brought too long a day;
But now, I often wish the night
Had borne my breath away!

I remember, I remember
The roses, red and white,
The violets, and the lily-cups,
Those flowers made of light!
The lilacs where the robin built,
And where my brother set
The laburnum on his birthday –
The tree is living yet!

I remember, I remember
Where I was used to swing,
And thought the air must rush as fresh
To swallows on the wing;
My spirit flew in feathers then,
That is so heavy now,
And summer pools could hardly cool
The fever on my brow!

I remember, I remember
The fir trees dark and high;
I used to think their slender tops
Were close against the sky:
It was a childish ignorance,
But now 'tis little joy
To know I'm farther off from heav'n
Than when I was a boy.

THOMAS HOOD (1799–1845)

The Fairies

Up the airy mountain,
    Down the rushy glen,
We daren't go a-hunting
    For fear of little men;
Wee folk, good folk,
    Trooping all together;
Green jacket, red cap,
    And white owl's feather!

Down along the rocky shore
    Some make their home,
They live on crispy pancakes
    Of yellow-tide foam;
Some in the reeds
    Of the black mountain lake,
With frogs for their watch-dogs
    All night awake.

High on the hilltop
    The old king sits;

He is now so old and grey
   He's nigh lost his wits.
With a bridge of white mist
   Columbkill he crosses,
On his stately journeys
   From Slieveleague to Rosses;
Or going up with music
   On cold starry nights,
To sup with the queen
   Of the gay Northern Lights.

They stole little Bridget
   For seven years long;
When she came down again
   Her friends were all gone.
They took her lightly back,
   Between the night and morrow,
They thought that she was fast asleep,
   But she was dead with sorrow.
They have kept her ever since
   Deep within the lakes,

On a bed of flag-leaves,
　Watching till she wakes.

By the craggy hillside,
　Through the mosses bare,
They have planted thorn-trees
　For pleasure here and there.
Is any man so daring
　As dig them up in spite,
He shall find their sharpest thorns
　In his bed at night.

Up the airy mountain,
　Down the rushy glen,
We daren't go a-hunting
　For fear of little men;
Wee folk, good folk,
　Trooping all together;
Green jacket, red cap,
　And white owl's feather!

WILLIAM ALLINGHAM (1824–89)

From a Railway Carriage

Faster than fairies, faster than witches,
Bridges and houses, hedges and ditches;
And charging along like troops in a battle,
All through the meadows, the horses and cattle;
All of the sights of the hill and the plain
Fly as thick as driving rain;
And ever again, in the wink of an eye,
Painted stations whistle by.

Here is a child who clambers and scrambles,
All by himself and gathering brambles;
Here is a tramp who stands and gazes;
And there is the green for stringing the daisies!
Here is a cart run away in the road,
Lumping along with man and load;
And here is a mill, and there is a river:
Each a glimpse and gone for ever!

ROBERT LOUIS STEVENSON (1850–94)

Midnight on the Great Western

In the third-class seat sat the journeying boy,
    And the roof-lamp's oily flame
Played down on his listless form and face,
Bewrapt past knowing to what he was going,
      Or whence he came.

In the band of his hat the journeying boy
    Had a ticket stuck; and a string
Around his neck bore the key of his box,
That twinkled gleams of the lamp's sad beams
      Like a living thing.

What past can be yours, O journeying boy,
    Towards a world unknown,
Who calmly, as if uncurious quite
On all at stake, can undertake
      This plunge alone?

Knows your soul a sphere, O journeying boy,
　　Our rude realms far above,
Whence with spacious vision you mark and mete
This region of sin that you find you in,
　　　　But are not of?

THOMAS HARDY (1840–1928)

Saturday Afternoon

From all the jails the boys and girls
Ecstatically leap –
Beloved, only afternoon
That prison doesn't keep.

They storm the earth and stun the air,
A mob of solid bliss –
Alas! that frowns should lie in wait
For such a foe as this!

EMILY DICKINSON (1830–86)

Going Downhill on a Bicycle

A BOY'S SONG

With lifted feet, hands still,
I am poised, and down the hill
Dart, with heedful mind;
The air goes by in a wind.

Swifter and yet more swift,
Till the heart with a mighty lift
Makes the lungs laugh, the throat cry,
'O bird, see; see, bird, I fly.

'Is this, is this your joy?
O bird, then I, though a boy,
For a golden moment share
Your feathery life in air!'

Say, heart, is there aught like this
In a world that is full of bliss?
'Tis more than skating, bound
Steel-shod to the level ground.

Speed slackens now, I float
Awhile in my airy boat;
Till, when the wheels scarce crawl,
My feet to the treadles fall.

Alas, that the longest hill
Must end in a vale; but still,
Who climbs with toil, wheresoe'er,
Shall find wings waiting there.

HENRY CHARLES BEECHING (1859–1919)

Youth

Oh, the wild joy of living: the leaping from rock
                           to rock,
The strong rending of boughs from the fir-trees, the
                           cool silver shock
Of the plunge in the pool's living water, the hunt of
                           the bear,
And the sultriness showing the lion is couch'd in his lair.
And the meal, the rich dates yellow'd over with
                           gold-dust divine,
And the locust fresh steeped in the pitcher, the full
                           draught of wine,
And the sleep in the dried river-channel where
                           bulrushes tell
That the water was wont to go warbling so softly and well.
How good is man's life, the mere living! how fit
                           to employ
All the heart and the soul and the senses for ever in joy!

ROBERT BROWNING (1812–89)

A Short Song of Congratulation

Long expected one-and-twenty,
Lingering year at last is flown:
Pomp and pleasure, pride and plenty,
Great Sir John, are all your own.

Loosened from the minor's tether,
Free to mortgage or to sell,
Wild as wind, and light as feather,
Bid the slaves of thrift farewell.

Call the Betties, Kates and Jennies,
Every name that laughs at care;
Lavish of your grandsire's guineas,
Show the spirit of an heir.

All that prey on vice and folly
Joy to see their quarry fly;
Here the gamester light and jolly,
There the lender grave and sly.

Wealth, Sir John, was made to wander,
Let it wander as it will;
See the jockey, see the pander,
Bid them come and take their fill.

When the bonny blade carouses,
Pockets full, and spirits high,
What are acres? What are houses?
Only dirt, or wet or dry.

If the guardian or the mother
Tell the woes of wilful waste,
Scorn their counsel, scorn their pother:
You can hang or drown at last!

DR SAMUEL JOHNSON (1709–84)

The Golden Rules of Conduct

Give thy thoughts no tongue,
Nor any unproportion'd thought his act.
Be thou familiar, but by no means vulgar.
Those friends thou hast, and their adoption tried,
Grapple them to thy soul with hoops of steel;
But do not dull thy palm with entertainment
Of each new-hatched, unfledged comrade. Beware
Of entrance to a quarrel, but being in,
Bear't that the opposed may beware of thee,
Give every man thy ear, but few thy voice:

Take each man's censure, but reserve thy judgment.
Costly thy habit as thy purse can buy,
But not express'd in fancy; rich, not gaudy;
For the apparel oft proclaims the man,
And they in France of the best rank and station
Are most select and generous chief in that.
Neither a borrower nor a lender be;
For loan oft loses both itself and friend,

And borrowing dulls the edge of husbandry.
This above all: to thine own self be true,
And it must follow, as the night the day,
Thou canst not then be false to any man.

WILLIAM SHAKESPEARE (1564–1616), *Hamlet*, 1, 3

The Retreat

Happy those early days! When I
Shined in my angel-infancy.
Before I understood this place
Appointed for my second race,
Or taught my soul to fancy aught
But a white, celestial thought;
When yet I had not walked above
A mile, or two, from my first love,
And looking back (at that short space)
Could see a glimpse of his bright face;
When on some gilded cloud, or flower,
My gazing soul would dwell an hour,

And in those weaker glories spy
Some shadows of eternity;
Before I taught my tongue to wound
My conscience with a sinful sound,
Or had the black art to dispense
A several sin to every sense,
But felt through all this fleshly dress
Blight shoots of everlastingness.
 O how I long to travel back
And tread again that ancient track!
That I might once more reach that plain,
Where first I left my glorious train,
From whence the enlightened spirit sees
That shady City of palm trees;
But (ah!) my soul with too much stay
Is drunk, and staggers in the way.
Some men a forward motion love,
But I by backward steps would move,
And when this dust falls to the urn,
In that state I came, return.

HENRY VAUGHAN (1621–93)

The Days of Wine and Roses

Vitae summa brevis spem
nos vetat incohare longam

They are not long, the weeping and the laughter,
　　Love and desire and hate:
I think they have no portion in us after
　　We pass the gate.

They are not long, the days of wine and roses:
　　Out of a misty dream
Our path emerges for a while, then closes
　　Within a dream.

ERNEST DOWSON (1867–1900)

To the Virgins, to Make Much of Time

Gather ye rosebuds while ye may,
    Old Time is still a flying;
And this same flower that smiles today,
    Tomorrow will be dying.

The glorious lamp of heaven, the sun,
    The higher he's a-getting;
The sooner will his race be run,
    And nearer he's to setting.

That age is best which is the first,
    When youth and blood are warmer;
But being spent, the worse, and worst
    Times, still succeed the former.

Then be not coy, but use your time,
    And while ye may, go marry;
For having lost but once your prime,
    You may for ever tarry.

ROBERT HERRICK (1591–1674)

Cynara

Non sum qualis eram bonae sub regno Cynarae

Last night, ah, yesternight, betwixt her lips and mine
There fell thy shadow, Cynara! thy breath was shed
Upon my soul between the kisses and the wine;
And I was desolate and sick of an old passion,
    Yea, I was desolate and bowed my head:
I have been faithful to thee, Cynara! in my fashion.

All night upon mine heart I felt her warm heart beat,
Night-long within mine arms in love and sleep she lay;
Surely the kisses of her bought red mouth were sweet;
But I was desolate and sick of an old passion,
    When I awoke and found the dawn was grey:
I have been faithful to thee, Cynara! in my fashion.

I have forgot much, Cynara! gone with the wind,
Flung roses, roses riotously with the throng,

Dancing, to put thy pale, lost lilies out of mind;
But I was desolate and sick of an old passion,
    Yea, all the time, because the dance was long:
I have been faithful to thee, Cynara! in my fashion.

I cried for madder music and for stronger wine,
But when the feast is finished and the lamps expire,
Then falls thy shadow, Cynara! the night is thine;
And I am desolate and sick of an old passion,
    Yea, hungry for the lips of my desire:
I have been faithful to thee, Cynara! in my fashion.

ERNEST DOWSON (1867–1900)

The World

The world is too much with us, late and soon,
Getting and spending, we lay waste our powers:
Little we see in nature that is ours;
We have given our hearts away, a sordid boon!

This sea that bares her bosom to the moon;
The winds that will be howling at all hours
And are up-gather'd now like sleeping flowers;
For this, for everything, we are out of tune;
It moves us not. Great God! I'd rather be
A pagan suckled in a creed outworn;
So might I, standing on this pleasant lea,
Have glimpses that would make me less forlorn;
Have sight of Proteus rising from the sea;
Or hear old Triton blow his wreathèd horn.

WILLIAM WORDSWORTH (1770–1850)

A Hundred Years Hence

Let us drink and be merry, dance, joke and rejoice,
With claret and sherry, theorbo and voice!
The changeable world to our joy is unjust,
   All treasure's uncertain,
   Then down with your dust!

In frolics dispose your pounds, shillings and pence,
For we shall be nothing a hundred years hence.

We'll sport and be free with Moll, Betty and Dolly,
Have oysters and lobsters to cure melancholy:
Fish-dinners will make a man spring like a flea,
   Dame Venus, love's lady,
    Was born of the sea:
With her and with Bacchus we'll tickle our sense,
For we shall be past it a hundred years hence.

Your most beautiful bride who with garlands is
                            crowned
And kills with each glance as she treads on the ground,
Whose lightness and brightness doth shine in
                             such splendour
   That none but the stars
   Are thought fit to attend her,
Though now she be pleasant and sweet to the sense,
Will be damnable mould a hundred years hence.

Then why should we turmoil in cares and in fears,
Turn all our tranquillity to sighs and to tears?
Let's eat, drink and play till the worms do corrupt us,
   'Tis certain, *Post mortem*
   Nulla voluptas.
For health, wealth and beauty, wit, learning and sense
Must all come to nothing a hundred years hence.

THOMAS JORDAN (1612–85)

Ozymandias

I met a traveller from an antique land
Who said: Two vast and trunkless legs of stone
Stand in the desert. Near them, on the sand,
Half sunk, a shattered visage lies, whose frown
And wrinkled lip and sneer of cold command
Tell that its sculptor well those passions read
Which yet survive, stamped on these lifeless things,
The hand that mocked them and the heart that fed;

And on the pedestal these words appear:
'My name is Ozymandias, king of kings:
Look on my works, ye mighty, and despair!'
Nothing beside remains. Round the decay
Of that colossal wreck, boundless and bare,
The lone and level sands stretch far away.

PERCY BYSSHE SHELLEY (1792–1822)

The Music Makers

We are the music makers
    And we are the dreamers of dreams,
Wandering by lone sea-breakers,
    And sitting by desolate streams;
Word losers and world forsakers
    On whom the pale moon gleams:
Yet we are the movers and shakers
    Of the world for ever, it seems.

With wonderful deathless ditties
We build up the world's great cities,
   And out of a fabulous story
   We fashion an empire's glory:
One man with a dream, at pleasure,
   Shall go forth and conquer a crown;
And these with a new song's measure
   Can trample an empire down.

We in the ages lying
   In the buried past of the earth,
Built Nineveh with our sighing
   And Babel itself with our mirth,
And o'erthrew them with prophesying
   To the old of the new world's worth:
For each age is a dream that is dying
   Or one that is coming to birth.

ARTHUR O'SHAUGHNESSY (1844–81)

The Beginning

Some day I shall rise and leave my friends
And seek you again through the world's far ends,
You whom I found so fair
(Touch of your hands and smell of your hair!),
My only god in the days that were.
My eager feet shall find you again,
Though the sullen years and the mark of pain
Have changed you wholly; for I shall know
(How could I forget having loved you so?),
In the sad half-light of evening,
The face that was all my sunrising.
So then at the ends of the earth I'll stand
And hold you fiercely by either hand,
And seeing your age and ashen hair
I'll curse the thing that once you were,
Because it is changed and pale and old
(Lips that were scarlet, hair that was gold!),

And I loved you before you were old and wise,
When the flame of youth was strong in your eyes
– And my heart is sick with memories.

RUPERT BROOKE (1887–1915)

The Kingdoms of the Earth Go by

The kingdoms of the earth go by
In purple and in gold:
They rise, they flourish, and they die,
And all their tale is told.
One kingdom only is divine,
One banner triumphs still:
Its king – a servant, and its sign –
A gibbet on a hill.

ANONYMOUS

The Wish

Well then; I now do plainly see,
This busy world and I shall ne'er agree;
The very honey of all earthly joy
Does of all meats the soonest cloy,
And they, methinks, deserve my pity,
Who for it can endure the stings,
The crowd, and buzz, and murmurings
Of this great hive, the city.

Ah, yet, ere I descend to th' grave
May I a small house and large garden have!
And a few friends, and many books, both true,
Both wise, and both delightful too!
And since love ne'er will from me flee,
A mistress moderately fair,
And good as guardian-angels are;
Only belov'd, and loving me!

ABRAHAM COWLEY (1618–67)

Don't We All

I often wish'd that I had clear,
For life, six hundred pounds a year,
A handsome house to lodge a friend,
A river at my garden's end.
A terrace walk, and half a rood
Of land, set out to plant a wood.

JONATHAN SWIFT (1667–1745)

Parting

The past is a strange land, most strange.
Wind blows not there, nor does rain fall:
If they do, they cannot hurt at all.
Men of all kinds as equals range

The soundless fields and streets of it.
Pleasure and pain there have no sting,

The perished self not suffering
That lacks all blood and nerve and wit,

And is in shadowland a shade.
Remembered joy and misery
Bring joy to the joyous equally;
Both sadden the sad. So memory made
Parting today a double pain:
First because it was parting; next
Because the ill it ended vexed
And mocked me from the past again,

Not as what had been remedied
Had I gone on – not that, oh no!
But as itself no longer woe;
Sighs, angry word and look and deed

Being faded: rather a kind of bliss,
For there spiritualised it lay
In the perpetual yesterday
That naught can stir or strain like this.

EDWARD THOMAS (1878–1917)

The First Day

I wish I could remember the first day,
First hour, first moment of your meeting me,
If bright or dim the season, it might be
Summer or winter for aught that I can say;
So unrecorded did it slip away,
So blind was I to see and to foresee,
So dull to mark the budding of my tree
That would not blossom yet for many a May,
If only I could recollect it, such
A day of days! I let it come and go
As traceless as a thaw of bygone snow;
It seemed to mean so little, meant so much;
If only now I could recall that touch,
First touch of hand in hand. Did one but know!

CHRISTINA ROSSETTI (1830–94)

The Choice

Grant me, indulgent heaven! a rural seat,
Rather contemptible than great!
Where, though I taste life's sweets, still I may be
Athirst for immortality!
I would have business; but exempt from strife!
A private, but an active life!
A conscience bold, and punctual to his charge!
My stock of health; or patience large!
Some books I'd have, and some acquaintance too!
But very good, and very few!
Then (if one mortal two such grants may crave!)
From silent life, I'd steal into my grave!

NAHUM TATE (1652–1715)

Farewell to Juliet

I see you, Juliet, still, with your straw hat
Loaded with vines, and with your dear pale face,
On which those thirty years so lightly sat,
And the white outline of your muslin dress.
You wore a little fichu trimmed with lace
And crossed in front, as was the fashion then,
Bound at your waist with a broad band or sash,
All white and fresh and virginally plain.
There was a sound of shouting far away
Down in the valley, as they called to us,
And you, with hands clasped seeming still to pray
Patience of fate, stood listening to me thus,
With heaving bosom. There a rose lay curled.
It was the reddest rose in all the world.

WILFRID BLUNT (1840–1922)

The Voice

Woman much missed, how you call to me, call to me,
Saying that now you are not as you were
When you had changed from the one who was all to me,
But as at first, when our day was fair.

Can it be you that I hear? Let me view you, then,
Standing as when I drew near to the town
Where you would wait for me: yes, as I knew you then,
Even to the original air-blue gown!

Or is it only the breeze, in its listlessness,
Travelling across the wet mead to me here,
You being ever dissolved to wan wistlessness,
Heard no more again far or near?

    Thus I; faltering forward,
    Leaves around me falling,
Wind oozing thin through the thorn from norward
    And the woman calling.

THOMAS HARDY (1840–1928)

Remembrance of Things Past

When to the sessions of sweet silent thought
I summon up remembrance of things past,
I sigh the lack of many a thing I sought,
And with old woes new wail my dear time's waste:
Then can I drown an eye unused to flow,
For precious friends hid in death's dateless night,
And weep afresh love's long since cancell'd woe,
And moan the expense of many a vanish'd sight:
Then can I grieve at grievances foregone
And heavily from woe to woe tell o'er
The sad account of fore-bemoanèd moan,
Which I new pay as if not paid before.
    But if the while I think on thee, dear friend,
    All losses are restored and sorrows end.

WILLIAM SHAKESPEARE (1564–1616)

Tears, Idle Tears

Tears, idle tears, I know not what they mean:
Tears from the depth of some divine despair
Rise in the heart, and gather to the eyes,
In looking on the happy autumn fields,
And thinking of the days that are no more.

Fresh as the first beam glittering on a sail,
That brings our friends up from the underworld,
Sad as the last which reddens over one
That sinks with all we love below the verge;
So sad, so fresh, the days that are no more.

Ah, sad and strange as in dark summer dawns
The earliest pipe of half-awakened birds
To dying ears, when unto dying eyes
The casement slowly grows a glimmering square;
So sad, so strange, the days that are no more.

Dear as remembered kisses after death,
And sweet as those by hopeless fancy feigned
On lips that are for others; deep as love,
Deep as first love, and wild with all regret;
O death in life, the days that are no more.

ALFRED, LORD TENNYSON (1809–92)

Let It be Forgotten

Let it be forgotten, as a flower is forgotten,
    Forgotten as a fire that once was singing gold,
Let it be forgotten for ever and ever,
    Time is a kind friend, he will make us old.

If anyone asks, say it was forgotten
Long and long ago,
As a flower, as a fire, as a hushed footfall
        In a long-forgotten snow.

SARA TEASDALE (1884–1933)

When All the World is Young

When all the world is young, lad,
    And all the trees are green;
And every goose a swan, lad,
    And every lass a queen;
Then hey for boot and horse, lad,
    And round the world away;
Young blood must have its course, lad,
    And every dog his day.

When all the world is old, lad,
    And all the trees are brown;
And all the sport is stale, lad,
    And all the wheels run down:
'Creep home and take your place there,
    The spent and maimed among:
God grant you find one face there
    You loved when all was young.

CHARLES KINGSLEY (1819–75)

The Old Familiar Faces

I have had playmates, I have had companions,
In my days of childhood, in my joyful schooldays,
All, all are gone, the old familiar faces.

I have been laughing, I have been carousing,
Drinking late, sitting late, with my bosom cronies,
All, all are gone, the old familiar faces.

I loved a love once, fairest among women:
Closed are her doors on me, I must not see her –
All, all are gone, the old familiar faces.

I have a friend, a kinder friend has no man;
Like an ingrate, I left my friend abruptly;
Left him, to muse on the old familiar faces.

Ghost-like I paced round the haunts of my
                                    childhood,

Earth seemed a desert I was bound to traverse,
Seeking to find the old familiar faces.

Friend of my bosom, thou more than a brother,
Why wert not thou born in my father's dwelling?
So might we talk of the old familiar faces –

How some they have died, and some they have
                              left me,
And some are taken from me; all are departed;
All, all are gone, the old familiar faces.

CHARLES LAMB (1775–1834)

O that 'twere Possible

O that 'twere possible
After long grief and pain
To find the arms of my true love
Round me once again! . . .

A shadow flits before me,
Not thou, but like to thee:
Ah, Christ! that it were possible
For one short hour to see
The souls we loved, that they might tell us
What and where they be!

ALFRED, LORD TENNYSON (1809–92)

Forebearance

Hast thou named all the birds without a gun?
Loved the wood-rose, and left it on its stalk?
At rich men's tables eaten bread and pulse?
Unarmed, faced danger with a heart of trust?
And loved so well a high behaviour,
In man or maid, that thou from speech refrained,
Nobility more nobly to repay?
O, be my friend, and teach me to be thine!

RALPH WALDO EMERSON (1803–82)

Revisiting the Old Home

I love the gracious littleness
   Of childhood's fancied reign:
The narrow chambers and the nooks
   That could a world contain;
The fairy landscapes on the walls
   And half-imagined faces:
The stairs from thoughtless steps fenced off,
   The landing – loved for races.

By strangers' feet the floors are trod
   That still in thought I see,
But the golden days of childhood
   May not return to me.

FRANCIS TURNER PALGRAVE (1824–97)

I Look into My Glass

I look into my glass,
And view my wasting skin,
And say, 'Would God it came to pass
My heart had shrunk as thin!'

For then, I, undistrest
By hearts grown cold to me,
Could lonely wait my endless rest
With equanimity.

But Time, to make me grieve.
Part steals, lets part abide;
And shakes this fragile frame at eve
With throbbings of noontide.

THOMAS HARDY (1840–1928)

Heraclitus

Εἶπέ τις, Ἡράκλειτε, τεὸν μόρον

They told me, Heraclitus, they told me you were dead;
They brought me bitter news to hear and bitter tears
                                    to shed.
I wept as I remembered how often you and I
Had tired the sun with talking and sent him down
                                    the sky.

And now that thou art lying, my dear old Carian guest,
A handful of grey ashes, long long ago at rest,
Still are thy pleasant voices, thy nightingales, awake,
For Death, he taketh all away, but them he cannot take.

WILLIAM JOHNSON CORY (1823–92)

Ah Me! The Little Battle's Done

Dispersed is all its chivalry;
Full many a move, since then, have we
'Mid life's perplexing chequers made,
And many a game with fortune played –
What is it we have won?
This, this at least – if this alone:
That never, never, never more,
As in those old still nights of yore
(Ere we were grown so sadly wise),
Can you and I shut out the skies,
Shut out the world, and wintry weather,
And, eyes exchanging warmth with eyes,
Play chess, as then we played, together!

EDWARD ROBERT BULWER-LYTTON (1831–91)

They Flee from Me

They flee from me that sometime did me seek
With naked foot, stalking in my chamber.
I have seen them gentle, tame, and meek,
That now are wild, and do not remember
That sometime they put themselves in danger
To take bread at my hand; and now they range
Busily seeking with a continual change.

Thanked be fortune, it hath been otherwise
Twenty times better; but once in special,
In thin array after a pleasant guise,
When her loose gown from her shoulders did fall
And she me caught in her arms long and small,
Therewithal sweetly did me kiss
And softly said, 'Dear heart, how like you this?'

It was no dream: I lay broad waking.
But all is turned, through my gentleness,

Into a strange fashion of forsaking.
And I have leave to go of her goodness,
And she also to use newfangleness.
But since that I so kindly am served
I would fain know what she hath deserved.

SIR THOMAS WYATT (1503–42)

Rondeau

Jenny kissed me when we met,
    Jumping from the chair she sat in;
Time, you thief! who love to get
    Sweets into your list, put that in.
Say I'm weary, say I'm sad;
    Say that health and wealth have missed me;
Say I'm growing old, but add –
    Jenny kissed me!

LEIGH HUNT (1784–1859)

Afterwards

When the present has latched its postern behind my
tremulous stay,
  And the May month flaps its glad green leaves
like wings,
Delicate-filmed as new-spun silk, will the neighbours say,
  'He was a man who used to notice such things'?

If it be in the dusk when, like an eyelid's soundless blink,
  The dewfall-hawk comes crossing the shades to alight
Upon the wind-warped upland thorn, a gazer may think,
  'To him this must have been a familiar sight.'

If I pass during some nocturnal blackness, mothy
and warm,
  When the hedgehog travels furtively over the lawn,
One may say, 'He strove that such innocent creatures,
should come to no harm,
  But he could do little for them; and now he is gone.'

If, when hearing that I have been stilled at last, they
                                            stand at the door,
   Watching the full-starred heavens that winter sees,
Will this thought rise on those who will meet my face
                                            no more,
   'He was one who had an eye for such mysteries'?

And will any say when my bell of quittance is heard in
                                            the gloom,
   And a crossing breeze cuts a pause in its outrollings,
Till they rise again, as they were a new bell's boom,
   'He hears it not now, but used to notice such things'?

THOMAS HARDY (1840–1928)

So We'll Go No More a-Roving

So we'll go no more a-roving
   So late into the night,
Though the heart be still as loving,
   And the moon be still as bright.

For the sword outwears its sheath,
   And the soul wears out the breast,
And the heart must pause to breathe,
   And love itself have rest.

Though the night was made for loving,
   And the day returns too soon,
Yet we'll go no more a-roving
   By the light of the moon.

GEORGE GORDON, LORD BYRON (1788–1824)

Heredity

I am the family face;
Flesh perishes, I live on,
Projecting trait and trace
Through time to times anon,
And leaping from place to place
Over oblivion.

The years-heired feature that can
In curve and voice and eye
Despise the human span
Of durance – that is I;
The eternal thing in man,
That heeds no call to die.

THOMAS HARDY (1840–1928)

Happy the Man

Happy the man, and happy he alone.
He who can call today his own –
He who, secure within, can say:
Tomorrow do thy worst, for I have lived today.
Come fair or foul, or rain, or shine,
The joys I have possessed, in spite of fate, are mine.
Not heaven itself over the past hath power;
But what has been has been, and I have had my hour.

JOHN DRYDEN (1631–1700)

Daisies are White

Daisies are white upon the churchyard sod,
    Sweet tears the clouds lean down and give:
The world is very lovely. O my God!
    I thank thee that I live.

ALEXANDER SMITH (1829–67)

Grow Old Along with Me!

Grow old along with me!
The best is yet to be,
The last of life, for which the first was made:
Our times are in His hand
Who saith, 'A whole I planned,
Youth shows but half; trust God: see all
                              nor be afraid!'

ROBERT BROWNING (1812–89)

Finis

I strove with none, for none was worth my strife,
    Nature I loved and, next to Nature, Art:
I warm'd both hands before the fire of life:
    It sinks, and I am ready to depart.

WALTER SAVAGE LANDOR (1775–1864)

At the Mid Hour of Night

At the mid hour of night, when stars are weeping, I fly
To the lone vale we loved, when life shone warm in
thine eye;
And I think that, if spirits can steal from the regions of air
To revisit past scenes of delight, thou wilt come to
me there,
And tell me our love is remembered even in the sky.

Then I sing the wild song it once was such rapture to hear,
When our voices commingling breathed like one on the ear;
And as Echo far off through the vale my sad orison rolls,
I think, O my love! 'tis thy voice from the kingdom
of souls
Faintly answering still the notes that once were so dear.

THOMAS MOORE (1779–1852)

Smiles on Harsh and Rugged Faces

The Optimist

I have seen smiles on harsh and rugged faces,
I have seen flowers in hard and stony places
And the Gold Cup won by the worst horse
                           in the races –
So I still hope.

ANONYMOUS

75

Philosophy

It might be easier
    To fail with land in sight,
Than gain my blue peninsular
    To perish of delight.

EMILY DICKINSON (1830–86)

The One Thing Needful

We may live without poetry, music, and art;
We may live without conscience and live without heart;
We may live without friends; we may live without books;
But civilised man cannot live without cooks.

He may live without lore – what is knowledge but grieving?
He may live without hope – what is hope but deceiving?
He may live without love – what is passion but pining?
But where is the man that can live without dining?

LORD LYTTON (1803–73)

Inviting a Friend to Supper

Tonight, grave sir, both my poor house and I
    Do equally desire your company:
Not that we think us worthy such a guest,
    But that your worth will dignify our feast
With those that come; whose grace may make
                           that seem
    Something which, else, could hope for no esteem.
It is the fair acceptance, sir, creates
    The entertainment perfect: not the cates.
Yet shall you have, to rectify your palate,
    An olive, capers, or some better sallade
Ush'ring the mutton; with a short-leg'd hen,
    If we can get her, full of eggs, and then,
Limons, and wine for sauce: to these, a coney
    Is not to be despaired of, for our money;
And, though fowl, now, be scarce, yet there are clerks,
    The sky not falling, think we may have larks.
I'll tell you of more, and lie, so you will come:

Of partrich, pheasant, woodcock, of which some
May yet be there; and godwit, if we can:
    Knat, rail, and ruffe too. How so'ere, my man
Shall read a piece of Virgil, Tacitus,
    Livy, or of some better book to us,
Of which we'll speak our minds, amidst our meat;
    And I'll profess no verses to repeat:
To this, if aught appear, which I not know of,
    That will the pastry, not my paper, show of.
Digestive cheese, and fruit there sure will be;
    But that, which most doth take my Muse, and me,
Is a pure cup of rich Canary wine,
    Which is the Mermaid's now, but shall be mine:
Of which had Horace, or Anacreon tasted,
    Their lives, as do their lines, till now had lasted.
Tobacco, Nectar, or the Thespian spring,
    Are all but Luther's beer, to this I sing.
Of this we will sup free, but moderately,
    And we will have no Pooly', or Parrot by;
Nor shall our cups make any guilty men:
    But, at our parting, we will be, as when

We innocently met. No simple word,
    That shall be utter'd at our mirthful board,
Shall make us sad next morning: or afright
    The liberty, that we'll enjoy tonight.

BEN JONSON (1572–1637)

Salad Dressing

To make this condiment your poet begs
The pounded yellow of two hard-boiled eggs;
Two boiled potatoes, passed through kitchen sieve,
Smoothness and softness to the salad give.
Let onion atoms lurk within the bowl,
And, half-suspected, animate the whole.
Of mordant mustard add a single spoon,
Distrust the condiment that bites so soon;
But deem it not, thou man of herbs, a fault
To add a double quantity of salt;

Four times the spoon with oil of Lucca crown,
And twice with vinegar procured from town;
And lastly o'er the flavoured compound toss
A magic soupçon of anchovy sauce.
Oh, green and glorious! Oh, herbaceous treat!
'Twould tempt the dying anchorite to eat;
Back to the world he'd turn his fleeting soul,
And plunge his fingers in the salad-bowl!
Serenely full, the epicure would say,
'Fate cannot harm me, I have dined today.'

SYDNEY SMITH (1771–1845)

Forbidden Fruit

Forbidden fruit a flavour has
    That lawful orchards mocks;
How luscious lies the pea within
    The pod that Duty locks!

EMILY DICKINSON (1830–86)

A Timely Consumption of Drink

There are people, I know, to be found,
    Who say, and apparently think,
That sorrow and care may be drowned
    By a timely consumption of drink.

Does not man, these enthusiasts ask,
    Most nearly approach the divine,
When engaged in the soul-stirring task
    Of filling his body with wine?

Have not beggars been frequently known,
    When satisfied, soaked and replete,
To imagine their bench was a throne
    And the civilised world at their feet?

Lord Byron has finely described
    The remarkably soothing effect
Of liquor, profusely imbibed,
    On a soul that is shattered and wrecked.

In short, if your body or mind
    Or your soul or your purse come to grief,
You need only get drunk, and you'll find
    Complete and immediate relief.

For myself, I have managed to do
    Without having recourse to this plan,
So I can't write a poem for you,
    And you'd better get someone who can.

JAMES KENNETH STEPHEN (1859–92)

Five Reasons We Should Drink

If all be true that I do think,
There are five reasons we should drink:
Good wine – a friend – or being dry –
Or lest we should be by and by –
Or any other reason why.

HENRY ALDRICH (1647–1710)

No More To Be Said

She tells me with claret she cannot agree,
And she thinks of a hogshead whene'er she sees me;
For I smell like a beast, and therefore must I
Resolve to forsake her, or claret deny.
Must I leave my dear bottle, that was always my friend,
And I hope will continue so to my life's end?
Must I leave it for her? 'Tis a very hard task:
Let her go to the devil! – bring the other full flask.

Had she taxed me with gaming, and bid me forbear,
'Tis a thousand to one I had lent her an ear:
Had she found out my Sally, up three pair of stairs,
I had balked her, and gone to St James's to prayers.
Had she bade me read homilies three times a day,
She perhaps had been humoured with little to say;
But, at night, to deny me my bottle of red,
Let her go to the devil! – there's no more to be said.

ANONYMOUS

Drinking

The thirsty earth soaks up the rain
And drinks and gapes for drink again.
The plants suck in the earth and are
With constant drinking fresh and fair.
The sea itself, which one would think
Should have but little need of drink,
Drinks ten thousand rivers up,
So fill'd that they or'eflow the cup.
The busy sun (and one would guess
By's drunken fiery face no less)
Drinks up the sea, and when h'as done,
The moon and stars drink up the sun.
They drink and dance by their own light,
They drink and revel all the night.
Nothing in nature's sober found,
But an eternal health goes round.
Fill up the bowl then, fill it high,
Fill all the glasses there, for why
Should every creature drink but I,
Why, Man of Morals, tell me why?

ABRAHAM COWLEY (1618–67)

The Sluggard

'Tis the voice of the sluggard; I hear him complain,
'You have wak'd me too soon, I must slumber again.'
As the door on its hinges, so he on his bed,
Turns his sides, and his shoulders, and his heavy head.
'A little more sleep and a little more slumber;'
Thus he wastes half his days and his hours
                                        without number;
And when he gets up, he sits folding his hands,
Or walks about sauntering, or trifling he stands.

ISAAC WATTS (1674–1748)

A Summing Up

I have lived and I have loved;
I have waked and I have slept;
I have sung and I have danced;
I have smiled and I have wept;

I have won and wasted treasure;
I have had my fill of pleasure;
And all these things were weariness,
And some of them were dreariness.
And all these things, but two things,
Were emptiness and pain:
And Love – it was the best of them;
And Sleep – worth all the rest of them.

CHARLES MACKAY (1814–89)

The Flea Asleep

My bed was such, as down nor feather can
Make one more soft, though Jove again turn swan;
No fear-distracted thoughts my slumbers broke,
I heard no screech owl shriek, nor raven croak;
Sleep's foe, the flea, that proud insulting elf,
Is now at truce, and is asleep itself.

SIR JOHN MENNES (1599–1671)

The Two Old Bachelors

Two old bachelors were living in one house;
One caught a muffin, the other caught a mouse.
Said he who caught the muffin to him who caught
                                    the mouse,
'This happens just in time, for we've nothing in the house
Save a tiny slice of lemon and a teaspoonful of honey,
And what to do for dinner – since we haven't any money?
And what can we expect if we haven't any dinner,
But to lose our teeth and eyelashes and keep on
                                    growing thinner?'
Said he who caught the mouse to him who caught
                                    the muffin,
'We might cook this little mouse if we only had
                                    some stuffin'!
If we had but sage and onions we could do extremely well,
But how to get that stuffin' it is difficult to tell!'

Those two old bachelors ran quickly to the town
And asked for sage and onions as they wandered
                                        up and down;
They borrowed two large onions, but no sage was to
                                        be found
In the shops or in the market or in all the gardens round.

But someone said, 'A hill there is, a little to the north,
And to its purpledicular top a narrow way leads forth;
And there among the rugged rocks abides an ancient sage,
An earnest man who reads all day a most perplexing page.
Climb up and seize him by the toes, all studious as he sits,
And pull him down, and chop him into endless little bits!
Then mix him with your onion (cut up likewise into
                                        scraps),
And your stuffin' will be ready, and very good – perhaps.'

Those two old bachelors, without loss of time,
The nearly purpledicular crags at once began to climb;

And at the top among the rocks, all seated in a nook,
They saw that sage a-wrestling with a most enormous book.
'You earnest sage!' aloud they cried, 'your book you've
                                        read enough in!
We wish to chop you into bits and mix you into stuffin'!'
But that old sage looked calmly up, and with his awful book
At those two bachelors' bald heads a certain aim he took;
All over crag and precipice they rolled promiscuous down,
At once they rolled and never stopped in lane or field
                                        or town;
And when they reached their house they found (besides
    their want of stuffin')
The mouse had fled – and previously had eaten up
                                        the muffin.

They left their home in silence by the once convivial door;
And from that hour those bachelors were never heard
                                        of more.

EDWARD LEAR (1812–88)

Our Photograph

She played me false, but that's not why
I haven't quite forgiven Di,
     Although I've tried:
This curl was hers, so brown, so bright,
She gave it me one blissful night,
     And – more beside!

In photo we were grouped together;
She wore the darling hat and feather
     That I adore;
In profile, by her side I sat,
Reading my poetry – but that
     She'd heard before.

Why, after all, Di threw me over
I never knew, and can't discover,
     Or even guess:

Maybe Smith's lyrics, she decided,
Were sweeter than the sweetest I did –
        I acquiesce.

A week before their wedding-day
When Smith was called in haste away
        To join the Staff,
Di gave to him, with tearful mien,
Our only photograph. I've seen
        That photograph.

I've seen it in Smith's album-book!
Just think! her hat – her tender look,
        And now that brute's!
Before she gave it, off she cut
My body, head and lyrics, but
She was obliged, the little slut,
        To leave my boots.

FREDERICK LOCKER-LAMPSON (1821–95)

91

The Tale of Lord Lovell

Lord Lovell he stood at his own front door,
    Seeking the hole for the key;
His hat was wrecked, and his trousers bore
    A rent across either knee,
When down came the beauteous Lady Jane
    In fair white draperie.

'Oh, where have you been, Lord Lovell?' she said.
    'Oh, where have you been?' said she;
'I have not closed an eye in bed,
    And the clock has just struck three.
Who has been standing you on your head
    In the ash-barrel, pardie?'

'I am not drunk, Lad' Shane,' he said,
    'And so late it cannot be;
The clock struck one as I enterèd –
    I heard it two times or three;

It must be the salmon on which I fed
    Has been too many for me.'

'Go tell your tale, Lord Lovell,' she said,
    'To the maritime cavalree,
To your grandmother of the hoary head –
    To anyone but me:
The door is not used to be openèd
    With a cigarette for a key.'

ANONYMOUS

The Latest Decalogue

Thou shalt have one God only; who
Would be at the expense of two?
No graven images may be
Worshipped, except the currency:
Swear not at all: for, for thy curse

Thine enemy is none the worse;
At church on Sunday to attend
Will serve to keep the world thy friend;
Honour thy parents: that is, all
From whom advancement may befall;
Thou shalt not kill: but need'st not strive
Officiously to keep alive;
Do not adultery commit:
Advantage rarely comes of it;
Thou shalt not steal: an empty feat,
When it's so lucrative to cheat;
Bear not false witness: let the lie
Have time on its own wings to fly;
Thou shalt not covet, but tradition
Approves all forms of competition.

ARTHUR HUGH CLOUGH (1819–1861)

The Ballad of William Bloat

In a mean abode in the Shankill Road
   Lived a man named William Bloat;
Now he had a wife, the plague of his life,
   Who continually got his goat,
And one day at dawn, with her night-shift on,
   He slit her bloody throat.

With a razor-gash he settled her hash –
   Oh, never was death so quick;
But the steady drop on the pillow slip
   Of her life-blood turned him sick,
And the pool of gore on the bedroom floor
   Grew clotted and cold and thick.

Now he was right glad he had done as he had
   As his wife lay there so still,
When a sudden awe of the mighty Law
   Struck his heart with an icy chill,

And, to finish the fun so well begun,
   He resolved himself to kill.

He took the sheet from his wife's cold feet
   And knotted it into a rope,
And hanged himself from the pantry shelf –
   An easy death, let's hope.
In the jaws of death with his latest breath
   Said he, 'To Hell with the Pope.'

But the strangest turn of the whole concern
   Is only just beginning:
He went to Hell, but his wife got well
   And is still alive and sinning,
For the razor-blade was Dublin-made
   But the sheet was Belfast linen.

ANONYMOUS

Wagner

Creeps in half wanton, half asleep,
   One with a fat wide hairless face.
He likes love-music that is cheap;
   Likes women in a crowded place;
     And wants to hear the noise they're making.

His heavy eyelids droop half-over,
   Great pouches swing beneath his eyes.
He listens, thinks himself the lover,
   Heaves from his stomach wheezy sighs;
     He likes to feel his heart's a-breaking.

The music swells. His gross legs quiver.
   His little lips are bright with slime.
The music swells. The women shiver.
   And all the while, in perfect time,
     His pendulous stomach hangs a-shaking.

RUPERT BROOKE (1887–1915)

How Pleasant to Know Mr Lear

How pleasant to know Mr Lear!
    Who has written such volumes of stuff!
Some think him ill-tempered and queer,
    But a few think him pleasant enough.

His mind is concrete and fastidious,
    His nose is remarkably big:
His visage is more or less hideous
    His beard it resembles a wig.

He has ears, and two eyes, and ten fingers,
    Leastways if you reckon two thumbs;
Long ago he was one of the singers,
    But now he is one of the dumbs.

He sits in a beautiful parlour,
    With hundreds of books on the wall
He drinks a great deal of Marsala,
    But never gets tipsy at all.

He has many friends, laymen and clerical,
  Old Foss is the name of his cat:
His body is perfectly spherical,
  He weareth a runcible hat.

When he walks in a waterproof white,
  The children run after him so!
Calling out, 'He's come out in his night-
  gown, that crazy old Englishman, oh!'

He weeps by the side of the ocean,
  He weeps on the top of the hill;
He purchases pancakes and lotion,
  And chocolate shrimps from the mill.

He reads but he cannot speak Spanish,
  He cannot abide ginger-beer:
Ere the days of his pilgrimage vanish,
  How pleasant to know Mr Lear!

EDWARD LEAR (1812–1888)

The Rainbow

My heart leaps up when I behold
    A rainbow in the sky:
So was it when my life began;
So is it now I am a man;
So be it when I shall grow old,
    Or let me die!
The child is father of the man;
And I could wish my days to be
Bound each to each by natural piety.

WILLIAM WORDSWORTH (1770–1850)

Triolet

'The child is father to the man.'
How can he be? The words are wild.
Suck any sense from that who can:
'The child is father to the man.'
No; what the poet did write ran,
'The man is father to the child.'
'The child is father to the man'!
How *can* he be? The words are wild.

GERARD MANLEY HOPKINS (1844–89)

Lucy

She dwelt among the untrodden ways
   Beside the springs of Dove,
A maid whom there were none to praise
   And very few to love:

A violet by a mossy stone
   Half hidden from the eye!
Fair as a star, when only one
   Is shining in the sky.

She lived unknown, and few could know
   When Lucy ceased to be;
But she is in her grave, and, oh,
   The difference to me!

WILLIAM WORDSWORTH (1770–1850)

Wordsworth Unvisited

He lived amidst th' untrodden ways
   To Rydal Lake that lead;
A bard whom there were none to praise,
   And very few to read.

Behind a cloud his mystic sense,
   Deep-hidden, who can spy?
Bright as the night when not a star
   Is shining in the sky.

Unread his works – his 'Milk White Doe'
   With dust is dark and dim;
It's still in Longman's shop, and oh!
   The difference to him!

HARTLEY COLERIDGE (1796–1849)

Epigram on the Feuds between Handel and Bononcini

Some say, compared to Bononcini,
That Mynheer Handel's but a ninny;
Others aver that he to Handel
Is scarcely fit to hold a candle:
Strange all this difference should be
'Twixt Tweedle-dum and Tweedle-dee!

JOHN BYROM (1692–1763)

On Donne's Poetry

With Donne, whose muse on dromedary trots,
Wreathe iron pokers into true-love knots;
Rhyme's sturdy cripple, fancy's maze and clue,
Wit's forge and fire-blast, meaning's press and screw.

SAMUEL TAYLOR COLERIDGE (1772–1834)

An Epitaph on Claudy Phillips, a Musician

Phillips! whose touch harmonious could remove
The pangs of guilty power and hapless love,
Rest here, distressed by poverty no more,
Here find that calm thou gav'st so oft before;
Sleep undisturbed within this peaceful shrine,
Till angels wake thee with a note like thine.

DR SAMUEL JOHNSON (1709–84)

Epigram Engraved on the Collar of a Dog which I Gave to His Royal Highness

I am His Highness' dog at Kew;
Pray tell me, sir, whose dog are you?

ALEXANDER POPE (1688–1744)

The Lady's Diary

Lectured by Pa and Ma o'er night,
Monday at ten quite vexed and jealous,
Resolved in future to be right,
And never listen to the fellows:
Stitched half a wristband, read the text,
Received a note from Mrs Racket:
I hate that woman, she sat next
All church-time to sweet Captain Clackit.

Tuesday got scolded, did not care,
The toast was cold, 'twas past eleven;
I dreamed the Captain through the air
On Cupid's wings bore me to heaven;
Pouted and dined, dressed, looked divine,
Made an excuse, got Ma to back it;
Went to the play, what joy was mine!
Talked loud and laughed with Captain Clackit.

Wednesday came down no lark so gay,
'The girl's quite altered,' said my mother;
Cried Dad, 'I recollect the day
When, dearee, thou wert such another.'
Danced, drew a landscape, skimmed a play,
In the paper read that widow Flackit
To Gretna Green had run away,
The forward minx, with Captain Clackit.

Thursday fell sick: 'Poor soul she'll die.'
Five doctors came with lengthened faces;
Each felt my pulse; 'Ah me,' cried I,
'Are these my promised loves and graces?'
Friday grew worse; cried Ma, in pain,
'Our day was fair, heaven do not black it;
Where's your complaint, love?' – 'In my brain.'
'What shall I give you?' – 'Captain Clackit.'

Early next morn a nostrum came
Worth all their cordials, balms and spices;

A letter, I had been to blame;
The Captain's truth brought on a crisis.
Sunday, for fear of more delays,
Of a few clothes I made a packet,
And Monday morn stepped in a chaise
And ran away with Captain Clackit.

CHARLES DIBDIN (1745–1814)

Somebody

Somebody being a nobody,
Thinking to look like a somebody,
Said that he thought me a nobody:
Good little somebody-nobody,
Had you not known me a somebody,
Would you have called me a nobody?

ALFRED, LORD TENNYSON (1809–92)

Disenchantment

It dropped so low in my regard
  I heard it hit the ground,
And go to pieces on the stones
  At bottom of my mind;

Yet blamed the fate that fractured, less
  Than I reviled myself
For entertaining plated wares
  Upon my silver shelf.

EMILY DICKINSON (1830–86)

The Bounds of Knowledge

He did the utmost bounds of knowledge find,
He found them not so large as was his mind.

ABRAHAM COWLEY (1618–67)

Brahma 1

If the red slayer think he slays,
    Or if the slain think he is slain,
They know not well the subtle ways
    I keep, and pass, and turn again.

Far or forgot to me is near;
    Shadow and sunlight are the same;
The vanish'd gods to me appear;
    And one to me are shame and fame.

They reckon ill who leave me out;
    When me they fly, I am the wings;
I am the doubter and the doubt,
    And I the hymn the Brahmin sings.

The strong gods pine for my abode,
    And pine in vain the sacred Seven;

But thou, meek lover of the good!
  Find me, and turn thy back on heaven.

RALPH WALDO EMERSON (1803–82)

Brahma 2

If the wild bowler thinks he bowls,
  Or if the batsman thinks he's bowled,
They know not, poor misguided souls,
  They too shall perish unconsoled.
I am the batsman and the bat,
  I am the bowler and the ball,
The umpire, the pavilion cat,
  The roller, pitch, and stumps, and all.

ANDREW LANG (1844–1912)

Some Hallucinations

He thought he saw an elephant,
  That practised on a fife:
He looked again, and found it was
  A letter from his wife.
'At length I realise,' he said,
  'The bitterness of life!'

He thought he saw a buffalo
  Upon the chimney-piece:
He looked again, and found it was
  His sister's husband's niece,
'Unless you leave this house,' he said,
  'I'll send for the police!'

He thought he saw a rattlesnake
  That questioned him in Greek:
He looked again, and found it was
  The middle of next week.

'The one thing I regret,' he said,
  'Is that it cannot speak!'

He thought he saw a banker's clerk
  Descending from the bus:
He looked again, and found it was
  A hippopotamus:
'If this should stay to dine,' he said,
  'There won't be much for us!'

LEWIS CARROLL (1832–98)

On Charles II

Here lies Our Sovereign Lord the King,
  Whose word no man relies on,
Who never said a foolish thing
  Nor ever did a wise one.

JOHN WILMOT, EARL OF ROCHESTER (1648–80)

Gaiety and Innocence

You talk of Gaiety and Innocence!
The moment when the fatal fruit was eaten,
They parted ne'er to meet again; and Malice
Has ever since been playmate to light Gaiety,
From the first moment when the smiling infant
Destroys the flower or butterfly he toys with,
To the last chuckle of the dying miser,
Who on his deathbed laughs his last to hear
His wealthy neighbour has become a bankrupt.

SIR WALTER SCOTT (1771–1832)

Epigram of Treason

Treason doth never prosper – what's the reason?
For if it prosper, none dare call it treason.

SIR JOHN HARINGTON (1561–1612)

Not I

Some like drink
   In a pint pot,
Some like to think;
   Some not.

Strong Dutch cheese,
   Old Kentucky Rye,
Some like these;
   Not I.

Some like Poe,
   And others like Scott,
Some like Mrs Stowe;
   Some not.

Some like to laugh,
   Some like to cry,
Some like chaff;
   Not I.

ROBERT LOUIS STEVENSON (1850–94)

The Vicar of Bray

In good King Charles's golden days,
 When loyalty no harm meant,
A furious high-church man I was,
 And so I gained preferment.
Unto my flock I daily preached,
 Kings are by God appointed,
And damned are those who dare resist,
 Or touch the Lord's anointed.
And this is law, I will maintain
 Unto my dying day, sir,
That whatsoever king shall reign,
 I will be Vicar of Bray, sir!

When royal James possessed the crown,
 And popery grew in fashion,
The penal law I hooted down,
 And read the declaration:
The Church of Rome I found would fit
 Full well my constitution,
And I had been a Jesuit,

But for the Revolution.
And this is law, etc.

When William our deliverer came,
    To heal the nation's grievance,
I turned the cat in pan again,
    And swore to him allegiance:
Old principles I did revoke,
    Set conscience at a distance
Passive obedience is a joke,
    A jest is non-resistance.
And this is law, etc.

When glorious Anne became our queen,
    The Church of England's glory,
Another face of things was seen,
    And I became a Tory:
Occasional conformists base
    I damned, and moderation,
And thought the church in danger was
    From such prevarication.
And this is law, etc.

When George in pudding time came o'er,
    And moderate men looked big, sir,
My principles I changed once more,
    And so became a Whig, sir:
And thus preferment I procured,
    From our faith's Great Defender,
And almost every day abjured
    The Pope, and the Pretender.
And this is law, etc.

The illustrious House of Hanover,
    And Protestant succession,
To these I lustily will swear,
    Whilst they can keep possession:
For in my faith and loyalty
    I never once will falter,
But George my lawful king shall be,
    Except the times should alter.
And this is law, etc.

ANONYMOUS

118

Character of George Villiers, Duke of Buckingham

A man so various, that he seemed to be
Not one, but all mankind's epitome.
Stiff in opinions, always in the wrong;
Was everything by starts, and nothing long:
But, in the course of one revolving moon,
Was chemist, fiddler, statesman, and buffoon;
Then all for women, painting, rhyming, drinking,
Besides ten thousand freaks that died in thinking.
Blest madman, who could every hour employ,
With something new to wish, or to enjoy!

Railing and praising were his usual themes;
And both (to show his judgement) in extremes:
So over violent, or over civil,
That every man, with him, was God or Devil.
In squandering wealth was his peculiar art:
Nothing went unrewarded, but desert.

Beggared by fools, whom still he found too late:
He had his jest, and they had his estate.

JOHN DRYDEN (1631–1700)

On Prince Frederick

Here lies Fred,
Who was alive and is dead:
Had it been his father,
I had much rather;
Had it been his brother,
Still better than another;
Had it been his sister,
No one would have missed her;
Had it been the whole generation,
So much the better for the nation:
But since 'tis only Fred,
Who was alive and is dead,
There's no more to be said.

ANONYMOUS

A True Maid

'No, no; for my virginity,
  When I lose that,' says Rose, 'I'll die.'
'Behind the elms last night,' cried Dick,
  'Rose, were you not extremely sick?'

MATTHEW PRIOR (1664–1721)

When Lovely Woman Stoops to Folly

When lovely woman stoops to folly
And finds too late that men betray,
What charm can soothe her melancholy,
What art can wash her guilt away?

The only art her guilt to cover,
To hide her shame from every eye,
To give repentance to her lover
And wring his bosom is – to die.

OLIVER GOLDSMITH (1728–74)

She was Poor but She was Honest

She was poor but she was honest,
    Victim of a rich man's game;
First he loved her, then he left her,
    And she lost her maiden name.

Then she hastened up to London,
    For to hide her grief and shame;
There she met another rich man,
    And she lost her name again.

See her riding in her carriage,
    In the park and all so gay
All the nibs and nobby persons
    Come to pass the time of day.

See them at the gay theátre
    Sitting in the costly stalls
With one hand she holds the programme,
    With the other strokes his hand.

See him have her dance in Paris
    In her frilly underclothes;
All those Frenchies there applauding
    When she strikes a striking pose.

See the little country village
    Where her aged parents live,
Though they drink champagne she sends them,
    Still they never can forgive.

In the rich man's arms she flutters
    Like a bird with a broken wing;
First he loved her, then he left her,
    And she hasn't got a ring.

See him in his splendid mansion
    Entertaining with the best
While the girl as he has ruined
    Entertains a sordid guest.

See him riding in his carriage
    Past the gutter where she stands;
He has made a stylish marriage
    While she wrings her ringless hands.

See him in the House of Commons
   Passing laws to put down crime,
While the victim of his passions
   Slinks away to hide her shame.

See her on the bridge at midnight,
   Crying, 'Farewell, faithless love!'
There's a scream, a splash – Good heavens!
   What is she a-doing of?

Then they dragged her from the river,
   Water from her clothes they wrung;
They all thought that she was drownded,
   But the corpse got up and sung:

'It's the same the whole world over;
   It's the poor as gets the blame,
It's the rich as gets the pleasure –
   Ain't it all a bleeding shame!'

ANONYMOUS

Dawn

(*On the train between Bologna and Milan, second class*)

Opposite me two Germans snore and sweat.
   Through sullen swirling gloom we jolt and roar.
We have been here for ever: even yet
   A dim watch tells two hours, two aeons, more.
The windows are tight-shut and slimy-wet
   With a night's foetor. There are two hours more;
Two hours to dawn and Milan; two hours yet.
   Opposite me two Germans sweat and snore . . .

One of them wakes, and spits, and sleeps again.
   The darkness shivers. A wan light through the rain
Strikes on our faces, drawn and white. Somewhere
   A new day sprawls; and, inside, the foul air
Is chill, and damp, and fouler than before . . .
   Opposite me two Germans sweat and snore.

RUPERT BROOKE (1887–1915)

The Village Schoolmaster

Beside yon straggling fence that skirts the way,
With blossomed furze unprofitably gay,
There, in his noisy mansion, skilled to rule,
The village master taught his little school;
A man severe he was, and stern to view,
I knew him well, and every truant knew;
Well had the boding tremblers learned to trace
The day's disasters in his morning face;
Full well they laughed, with counterfeited glee,
At all his jokes, for many a joke had he:
Full well the busy whisper, circling round,
Conveyed the dismal tidings when he frowned;
Yet he was kind, or, if severe in aught,
The love he bore to learning was in fault;
The village all declared how much he knew;
'Twas certain he could write, and cipher too;
Lands he could measure, terms and tides presage,
And even the story ran that he could gauge.

In arguing, too, the parson owned his skill,
For, even though vanquished, he could argue still;
While words of learnèd length and thundering sound
Amazed the gazing rustics ranged around;
And still they gazed, and still the wonder grew
That one small head could carry all he knew.

OLIVER GOLDSMITH (1730–74)
from *The Deserted Village*

After Emerson

Lives of great men all remind us
As we o'er their pages turn,
That we too may leave behind us
Letters that we ought to burn.

ANONYMOUS

Delight in Disorder

A sweet disorder in the dress
Kindles in clothes a wantonness:
A lawn about the shoulders thrown
Into a fine distraction;
An erring lace, which here and there
Enthrals the crimson stomacher;
A cuff neglectful, and thereby
Ribbands to flow confusedly;
A winning wave (deserving note)
In the tempestuous petticoat;
A careless shoestring, in whose tie
I see a wild civility:
Do more bewitch me, than when art
Is too precise in every part.

ROBERT HERRICK (1591–1674)

A Touch of Blue

I always thought a touch of blue
Improved a charming woman's stocking.

R. MONKTON MILNES (1809–85)

Women's Degrees

A tangled web indeed we weave
When Adam grants degrees to Eve:
And much I doubt, had Eve first had 'em,
If she'd have done as much for Adam.

A. D. GODLEY (1856–1925)

You are Old, Father William

'You are old, Father William,' the young man said,
'And your hair has become very white;
And yet you incessantly stand on your head –
Do you think, at your age, it is right?'

'In my youth,' Father William replied to his son,
'I feared it might injure the brain;
But now that I'm perfectly sure I have none,
Why, I do it again and again.'

'You are old,' said the youth, 'as I mentioned before,
And have grown most uncommonly fat;
Yet you turned a back-somersault in at the door –
Pray, what is the reason of that?'

'In my youth,' said the sage, as he shook his grey locks,
'I kept all my limbs very supple
By the use of this ointment – one shilling the box –
Allow me to sell you a couple.'

For anything tougher than suet;
Yet you finished the goose, with the bones and the beak –
Pray, how did you manage to do it?'

'In my youth,' said his father, 'I took to the law,
And argued each case with my wife;
And the muscular strength which it gave to my jaw
Has lasted the rest of my life.'

'You are old,' said the youth; 'one would hardly suppose
That your eye was as steady as ever;
Yet you balanced an eel on the end of your nose –
What made you so awfully clever?'

'I have answered three questions, and that is enough,'
Said his father; 'don't give yourself airs!
Do you think I can listen all day to such stuff?
Be off, or I'll kick you downstairs!'

LEWIS CARROLL (1832–98)

Canopus

When quacks with pills political would dope us,
    When politics absorbs the livelong day,
I like to think about the star Canopus,
    So far, so far away.

Greatest of visioned suns, they say who list 'em;
    To weigh it science always must despair.
Its shell would hold our whole dinged solar system,
    Nor ever know 'twas there.

When temporary chairmen utter speeches,
    And frenzied henchmen howl their battle hymns,
My thoughts float out across the cosmic reaches
    To where Canopus swims.

When men are calling names and making faces,
    And all the world's ajangle and ajar,
I meditate on interstellar spaces
    And smoke a mild seegar.

For after one has had about a week of
   The arguments of friends as well as foes,
A star that has no parallax to speak of
   Conduces to repose.

B. L. TAYLOR (1866–1921)

Wishes of an Elderly Man

I wish I loved the human race;
I wish I loved its silly face;
I wish I liked the way it walks;
I wish I liked the way it talks;
And when I'm introduced to one
I wish I thought, What jolly fun!

WALTER RALEIGH (1861–1922)

The Mouse's Petition

Oh! hear a pensive captive's prayer,
For liberty that sighs;
And never let thine heart be shut
Against the prisoner's cries.

For here forlorn and sad I sit,
Within the wiry grate;
And tremble at th' approaching morn,
Which brings impending fate.

If e'er thy breast with freedom glowed,
And spurned a tyrant's chain,
Let not thy strong oppressive force
A free-born mouse detain.

Oh! do not stain with guiltless blood
Thy hospitable hearth;
Nor triumph that thy wiles betrayed
A prize so little worth.

The scattered gleanings of a feast
My scanty meals supply;

But if thine unrelenting heart
That slender boon deny,

The cheerful light, the vital air,
Are blessings widely given;
Let nature's commoners enjoy
The common gifts of heaven.

The well-taught philosophic mind
To all compassion gives;
Casts round the world an equal eye,
And feels for all that lives.

If mind, as ancient sages taught,
A never-dying flame,
Still shifts through matter's varying forms,
In every form the same,

Beware, lest in the worm you crush
A brother's soul you find;
And tremble lest thy luckless hand
Dislodge a kindred mind.

Or, if this transient gleam of day
Be *all* of life we share,

Let pity plead within thy breast
That little *all* to spare.

So may thy hospitable board
With health and peace be crowned;
And every charm of heartfelt ease
Beneath thy roof be found.

So, when unseen destruction lurks,
Which mice like men may share,
May some kind angel clear thy path,
And break the hidden snare.

ANNA LAETITIA BARBAULD (1743–1825)

In Peterborough Churchyard

Reader, pass on, nor idly waste your time
In bad biography, or bitter rhyme;
For what I am, this cumbrous clay ensures,
And what I was is no affair of yours.

ANONYMOUS

Hairs Cast Their Shadows

The lowest trees have tops, the ant her gall,
The fly her spleen, the little spark his heat;
Hairs cast their shadows, though they be but small,
And bees have stings, although they be not great.
Seas have their source, and so have shallow springs,
And love is love, in beggars and in kings.
The ermine hath the fairest skin on earth,
Yet doth she choose the weasel for her peer;
The panther hath a sweet perfumed breath,
Yet doth she suffer apes to draw her near.
No flower more fresh than is the damask rose,
Yet next her side the nettle often grows.
Where waters smoothest run, deep'st are the fords,
The dial stirs, though none perceive it move;
The fairest faith is in the sweetest words,
The turtles sing not love, and yet they love.
True hearts have eyes and ears, no tongues to speak,
They hear and see, and sigh, and then they break.

SIR EDWARD DYER (*c.*1545–1607)

Lines Composed in a Wood on a Windy Day

My soul is awakened, my spirit is soaring,
And carried aloft on the wings of the breeze;
For above and around me, the wild wind is roaring
Arousing to rapture the earth and the seas.

The long withered grass in the sunshine is glancing,
The bare trees are tossing their branches on high;
The dead leaves beneath them are merrily dancing,
The white clouds are scudding across the blue sky.

I wish I could see how the ocean is lashing
The foam of its billows in whirlwinds of spray,
I wish I could see how its proud waves are dashing
And hear the wild roar of their thunder today!

ANNE BRONTË (1820–49)

Youthful Pleasures Still Delight Me

My head is grey, my blood is young,
Red, leaping in my veins:
The spring doth stir my spirit yet
To seek the cloistered violet,
The primrose in the lanes.
In heart I am a very boy,
Haunting the woods, the waterfalls,
The ivies on grey castle walls:
Weeping in silent joy
When the broad sun goes down to rest:

Or trembling o'er a sparrow's nest.
The world might laugh were I to tell
What most my old age cheers –
Memories of stars and crescent moons,
Of nutting strolls through autumn noons,
Rainbows 'mong April's tears.
But chief to live that hour again
When first I stood on sea-beach old,

First heard the voice, first saw unrolled
The glory of the main.

ALEXANDER SMITH (1830–67)

The Year's Awakening

How do you know that the pilgrim track
Along the belting zodiac
Swept by the sun in his seeming rounds
Is traced by now to the Fishes' bounds
And into the Ram, when weeks of cloud
Have wrapt the sky in a clammy shroud,
And never as yet a tint of spring
Has shown in the Earth's apparelling;
   O vespering bird, how do you know?
      How do you know?

How do you know, deep underground,
Hid in your bed from sight and sound,

Without a turn in temperature,
With weather life can scarce endure,
That light has won a fraction's strength,
And day put on some moments' length,
Whereof in merest rote will come,
Weeks hence, mild airs that do not numb.
  O crocus root, how do you know,
    How do you know?

THOMAS HARDY (1840–1928)

The Tulip

She slept beneath a tree
    Remembered but by me.
I touched her cradle mute:
She recognised the foot,
Put on her carmaine suit –
    And see!

EMILY DICKINSON (1830–86)

Spring

Nothing is so beautiful as spring –
   When weeds, in wheels, shoot long and lovely
                              and lush;
   Thrush's eggs look little low heavens, and thrush
Through the echoing timber does so rinse and wring
The ear, it strikes like lightnings to hear him sing;
   The glassy pear tree leaves and blooms, they brush
   The descending blue; that blue is all in a rush
With richness; the racing lambs too have fair
                            their fling.

What is all this juice and all this joy?
   A strain of the earth's sweet being in the beginning
In Eden garden. – Have, get, before it cloy,
   Before it cloud, Christ, lord, and sour with sinning,
Innocent mind and Mayday in girl and boy,
   Most, O maid's child, thy choice and worthy
                            the winning.

GERARD MANLEY HOPKINS (1844–89)

I So Liked Spring

I so liked spring last year
Because you were here;
The thrushes too –
Because it was these you so liked to hear.
I so liked you.

This year's a different thing –
I'll not think of you.
But I'll like spring because it is simply spring
As the thrushes do.

CHARLOTTE MEW (1869–1928)

Presentiment

Presentiment is that long shadow on the lawn
Indicative that suns go down;
The notice to the startled grass
That darkness is about to pass.

EMILY DICKINSON (1830–86)

Pippa's Song

The year's at the spring,
And day's at the morn;
Morning's at seven;
The hillside's dew-pearl'd;
The lark's on the wing;
The snail's on the thorn;
God's in His heaven –
All's right with the world!

ROBERT BROWNING (1812–89)

To Daffodils

Fair daffodils, we weep to see
    You haste away so soon:
As yet the early-rising sun
    Has not attained his noon.

Stay, stay,
  Until the hasting day
    Has run
  But to the evensong,
And, having prayed together, we
  Will go with you along.

We have short time to stay as you,
  We have as short a spring;
As quick a growth to meet decay
  As you, or anything.
    We die,
  As your hours do, and dry
    Away,
  Like to the summer's rain,
Or as the pearls of morning's dew,
  Ne'er to be found again.

ROBERT HERRICK (1591–1674)

Green Cornfield

The earth was green, the sky was blue:
  I saw and heard one sunny morn
A skylark hang between the two,
  A singing speck above the corn;

A stage below, in gay accord,
  White butterflies danced on the wing,
And still the singing skylark soared,
  And silent sank and soared to sing.

The cornfield stretched a tender green
  To right and left beside my walks;
I knew he had a nest unseen
  Somewhere among the million stalks.

And as I paused to hear his song
  While swift the sunny moments slid,
Perhaps his mate sat listening long,
  And listened longer than I did.

CHRISTINA ROSSETTI (1830–94)

A London Plane Tree

Green is the plane tree in the square,
　The other trees are brown;
They droop and pine for country air;
　The plane tree loves the town.

Here, from my garret-pane, I mark
　The plane tree bud and blow,
Shed her recuperative bark
　And spread her shade below.

Among her branches, in and out,
　The city breezes play;
The dun fog wraps her round about;
　Above, the smoke curls grey.

Others the country take for choice,
　And hold the town in scorn;
But she has listened to the voice
　On city breezes born.

AMY LEVY (1861–89)

The Beanfield

A beanfield in blossom smells as sweet
As araby, or groves of orange flowers;
Black-eyed and white, and feathered to one's feet,
How sweet they smell in morning's dewy hours.
When soothing night is left upon the flowers,
Another morn's sun shines brightly o'er the field,
And bean bloom glitters in the gems of showers,
And sweet the fragrance which the union yields
To battered footpaths crossing o'er the fields.

JOHN CLARE (1793–1864)

The Poplar Field

The poplars are fell'd, farewell to the shade
And the whispering sound of the cool colonnade,
The winds play no longer and sing in the leaves,
Nor Ouse on his bosom their image receives.

Twelve years have elaps'd since I last took a view
Of my favourite field and the bank where they grew,
And now in the grass behold they are laid,
And the tree is my seat that once lent me a shade.

The blackbird has fled to another retreat
Where the hazels afford him a screen from the heat,
And the scene where his melody charm'd me before,
Resounds with his sweet-flowing ditty no more.

My fugitive years are all hasting away,
And I must ere long lie as lowly as they,
With a turf on my breast, and a stone at my head,
Ere another such grove shall arise in its stead.

'Tis a sight to engage me, if anything can,
To muse on the perishing pleasures of man;
Though his life be a dream, his enjoyments, I see,
Have a being less durable even than he.

WILLIAM COWPER (1731–1800)

Fair Summer Droops

Fair summer droops, droop men and beasts therefore;
So fair a summer look for never more!
All good things vanish less than in a day,
Peace, plenty, pleasure, suddenly decay.
    Go not yet away, bright soul of the sad year,
    The earth is hell when thou leav'st to appear.

What, shall those flowers that decked thy garland erst,
Upon thy grave be wastefully dispersed?
O trees, consume your sap in sorrow's source;
Streams, turn to tears your tributary course.
    Go not yet hence, bright soul of the sad year,
    The earth is hell when thou leav'st to appear.

THOMAS NASHE (1567–c.1601)

Summer Evening

The frog, half fearful, jumps across the path,
And little mouse that leaves its hole at eve
Nimbles with timid dread beneath the swath;
My rustling steps awhile their joys deceive,
Till past – and then the cricket sings more strong,
And grasshoppers in merry moods still wear
The short night weary with their fretting song.
Up from behind the mole-hill jumps the hare,
Cheat of his chosen bed, and from the bank
The yellowhammer flutters in short fears
From off its nest hid in the grasses rank,
And drops again when no more noise it hears.
Thus nature's human link and endless thrall,
Proud man, still seems the enemy of all.

JOHN CLARE (1793–1864)

To Autumn

Season of mists and mellow fruitfulness!
    Close bosom-friend of the maturing sun;
Conspiring with him how to load and bless
    With fruit the vines that round the thatch-eaves run;
To bend with apples the mossed cottage-trees,
    And fill all fruit with ripeness to the core;
        To swell the gourd, and plump the hazel shells
    With a sweet kernel; to set budding more,
And still more, later flowers for the bees,
Until they think warm days will never cease,
        For summer has o'er-brimmed their clammy cells.

Who hath not seen thee oft amid thy store?
    Sometimes whoever seeks abroad may find
Thee sitting careless on a granary floor,
    Thy hair soft-lifted by the winnowing wind,
Or on a half-reaped furrow sound asleep,
    Drowsed with the fume of poppies, while thy hook

Spares the next swath and all its twinèd flowers;
And sometimes like a gleaner thou dost keep
   Steady thy laden head across a brook;
   Or by a cider-press, with patient look,
      Thou watchest the last oozings hours by hours.

Where are the songs of spring? Ay, where are they?
   Think not of them, thou hast thy music too –
While barred clouds bloom the soft-dying day,
   And touch the stubble-plains with rosy hue;
Then in a wailful choir the small gnats mourn
   Among the river sallows, borne aloft
      Or sinking as the light wind lives or dies;
And full-grown lambs loud bleat from hilly bourn;
   Hedge-crickets sing; and now with treble soft
   The redbreast whistles from a garden-croft;
      And gathering swallows twitter in the skies.

JOHN KEATS (1795–1821)

Autumn

Therefore their latter journey to the grave
Was like those days of later autumn tide
When he who in some town may chance to bide
Opens the window for the balmy air,
And seeing the golden hazy sky so fair,
And from some city garden hearing still
The wheeling rooks the air with music fill
Sweet hopeful music, thinketh: Is this spring?
Surely the year can scarce be perishing?
But then he leaves the clamour of the town,
And sees the scanty withered leaves fall down,
The half-ploughed field, the flowerless garden plot,
The dark full stream by summer long forgot,
The tangled hedges where, relaxed and dead,
The twining plants their withered berries shed,
And feels therewith the treachery of the sun,
And knows the pleasant time is well nigh done.

WILLIAM MORRIS (1834–96)

154

Fall, Leaves, Fall

Fall, leaves, fall; die, flowers, away;
Lengthen night, and shorten day!
Every leaf speaks bliss to me,
Fluttering from the autumn tree.

I shall smile when wreaths of snow
Blossom where the rose should grow;
I shall sing when night's decay
Ushers in a drearier day.

EMILY BRONTË (1818–48)

Thaw

Over the land freckled with snow half-thawed,
The speculating rooks at their nests cawed
And saw from elm-tops, delicate as flowers of grass,
What we below could not see – winter pass.

EDWARD THOMAS (1878–1917)

Winter

The small wind whispers through the leafless hedge
   Most sharp and chill, where the light snowy flakes
Rest on each twig and spike of wither'd sedge,
   Resembling scatter'd feathers; vainly breaks
The pale split sunbeam through the frowning cloud,
   On winter's frowns below – from day to day
Unmelted still he spreads his hoary shroud,
   In dithering pride on the pale traveller's way,
Who, croodling, hastens from the storm behind
Fast gathering deep and black, again to find
   His cottage fire and corner's sheltering bounds;
Where, haply, such uncomfortable days
   Make musical the wood-sap's frizzling sounds,
And hoarse loud bellows puffing up the blaze.

JOHN CLARE (1793–1864)

That Time of Year

That time of year thou mayst in me behold
When yellow leaves, or none, or few, do hang
Upon those boughs which shake against the cold,
Bare ruined choirs, where late the sweet birds sang.
In me thou see'st the twilight of such day
As after sunset fadeth in the west;
Which by and by black night doth take away,
Death's second self, that seals up all in rest.
In me thou see'st the glowing of such fire,
That on the ashes of his youth doth lie,
As the deathbed whereon it must expire,
Consumed with that which it was nourished by.
   This thou perceivest, which makes thy love more strong,
   To love that well which thou must leave ere long.

WILLIAM SHAKESPEARE (1564–1616)

Have You?

Have you seen but a bright lily grow
   Before rude hands have touched it?
Have you marked but the fall of the snow
   Before the soil hath smutched it?
Have you felt the wool of the beaver,
   Or swan's down ever?
Or have smelt o' the bud of the brier,
   Or the nard in the fire?
Or have tasted the bag of the bee?
O so white: O so soft, O so sweet is she!

BEN JONSON (1572–1637)

I Never Pluck the Rose

It is and ever was my wish and way
To let all flowers live freely, and all die
Whene'er their Genius bids their souls depart
Among their kindred in their native place.
I never pluck the rose: the violet's head
Hath shaken with my tread upon its bank
And not reproacht me: the ever sacred cup
Of the pure lily hath between my hands
Felt safe, unsoiled, nor lost one grain of gold.

WALTER SAVAGE LANDOR (1775–1864)

The Caterpillar

Brown and furry
Caterpillar in a hurry,
Take your walk
To the shady leaf, or stalk,
Or what not,
Which may be the chosen spot.
No toad to spy you,
Hovering bird of prey pass by you;
Spin and die
To live again a butterfly.

CHRISTINA ROSSETTI (1830–94)

The Pedigree of Honey

The pedigree of honey
Does not concern the bee;
A clover, any time, to him
Is aristocracy.

EMILY DICKINSON (1830–86)

The Sick Rose

O Rose, thou art sick!
The invisible worm
That flies in the night,
In the howling storm,
Has found out thy bed
Of crimson joy,
And his dark secret love
Does thy life destroy.

WILLIAM BLAKE (1757–1827)

The Fly

Little fly,
Thy summer's play
My thoughtless hand
Has brushed away.

Am not I
A fly like thee?
Or art not thou
A man like me?

For I dance
And drink and sing,
Till some blind hand
Shall brush my wing.

If thought is life
And strength and breath,
And the want
Of thought is death,

Then am I
A happy fly
If I live
Or if I die.

WILLIAM BLAKE (1757–1827)

The Grasshopper and the Cricket

The poetry of earth is never dead:
When all the birds are faint with the hot sun,
And hide in cooling trees, a voice will run
From hedge to hedge about the new-mown mead:
This is the grasshopper's – he takes the lead
In summer luxury – he has never done
With his delights, for when tired out with fun,
He rests at ease beneath some pleasant weed.
The poetry of earth is ceasing never:
On a lone winter evening, when the frost
Has wrought a silence, from the stove there shrills
The cricket's song, in warmth increasing ever,
And seems to one in drowsiness half lost
The grasshopper's among the grassy hills.

JOHN KEATS (1795–1821)

A Noiseless Patient Spider

A noiseless patient spider,
I mark'd where on a little promontory it stood
                              isolated,
Mark'd how, to explore the vacant vast surrounding,
It launch'd forth filament, filament, filament, out
                              of itself,
Ever unreeling them, ever tirelessly speeding them.

And you, O my soul, where you stand,
Surrounded, detached, in measureless oceans of space,
Ceaselessly musing, venturing, throwing, seeking
                    the spheres to connect them,
Till the bridge you will need be form'd, till the ductile
                              anchor hold,
Till the gossamer thread you fling catch somewhere,
                              O my soul.

WALT WHITMAN (1819–92)

Hiawatha's Brothers

Then the little Hiawatha
Learned of every bird its language,
Learned their names and all their secrets,
How they built their nest in summer,
Where they hid themselves in winter,
Talked with them whene'er he met them,
Called them 'Hiawatha's chickens'.
Of all beasts he learned the language,
Learned their names and all their secrets,
How the beavers built their lodges,
Where the squirrels hid their acorns,
How the reindeer ran so swiftly,
Why the rabbit was so timid,
Talked with them whene'er he met them,
Called them 'Hiawatha's brothers'.

HENRY WADSWORTH LONGFELLOW (1807–82)
FROM *The Song of Hiawatha*

Mouse's Nest

I found a ball of grass among the hay
And progged it as I passed and went away;
And when I looked I fancied something stirred,
And turned again and hoped to catch the bird –
When out an old mouse bolted in the wheats
With all her young ones hanging at her teats;
She looked so odd and so grotesque to me,
I ran and wondered what the thing could be,
And pushed the knapweed bunches where I stood;
Then the mouse hurried from the craking brood.
The young ones squeaked, and as I went away
She found her nest again among the hay.
The water o'er the pebbles scarce could run
And broad old cesspools glittered in the sun.

JOHN CLARE (1793–1864)

The Tiger

Tiger! Tiger! burning bright
In the forests of the night,
What immortal hand or eye
Could frame thy fearful symmetry?

In what distant deeps or skies
Burnt the fire of thine eyes?
On what wings dare he aspire?
What the hand dare seize the fire?

And what shoulder, and what art
Could twist the sinews of thy heart?
And, when thy heart began to beat,
What dread hand? and what dread feet?

What the hammer? what the chain?
In what furnace was thy brain?
What the anvil? what dread grasp
Dare its deadly terrors clasp?

When the stars threw down their spears,
And water'd heaven with their tears,
Did he smile his work to see?
Did he who made the lamb make thee?

Tiger! Tiger! burning bright
In the forests of the night,
What immortal hand or eye
Dare frame thy fearful symmetry?

WILLIAM BLAKE (1757–1827)

To a Goose

If thou didst feed on western plains of yore;
Or waddle wide with flat and flabby feet
Over some Cambrian mountain's plashy moor;
Or find in farmer's yard a safe retreat
From gypsy thieves, and foxes sly and fleet;
If thy grey quills, by lawyer guided, trace

Deeds big with ruin to some wretched race,
Or lovesick poet's sonnet, sad and sweet,
Wailing the rigour of his lady fair;
Or if, the drudge of housemaid's daily toil,
Cobwebs and dust thy pinions white besoil,
Departed Goose! I neither know nor care.
But this I know, that we pronounced thee fine,
Seasoned with sage and onions, and port wine.

ROBERT SOUTHEY (1774–1843)

The Windhover

I caught this morning morning's minion, king-
   dom of daylight's dauphin, dapple-dawn-drawn
                 Falcon, in his riding
   Of the rolling level underneath him steady air, and striding

High there, how he rung upon the rein of a
                                    wimpling wing
In his ecstasy! then off, off forth on swing,
   As a skate's heel sweeps smooth on a bow-bend:
                              the hurl and gliding
      Rebuffed the big wind. My heart in hiding
Stirred for a bird, – the achieve of, the mastery of
                                       the thing!

Brute beauty and valour and act, oh, air, pride,
                                    plume, here
   Buckle! AND the fire that breaks from thee then,
                                 a billion
Times told lovelier, more dangerous, O my chevalier!

   No wonder of it: shéer plód makes plough
                              down sillion
Shine, and blue-bleak embers, ah my dear,
   Fall, gall themselves, and gash gold-vermilion.

                        GERARD MANLEY HOPKINS (1844–89)

                              170

The Lark Now Leaves His Watery Nest

The lark now leaves his watery nest,
   And climbing, shakes his dewy wings:
He takes this window for the east;
   And to implore your light, he sings.
Awake, awake, the morn will never rise
Till she can dress her beauty at your eyes.

The merchant bows unto the seaman's star,
   The ploughman from the sun his season takes;
But still the lover wonders what they are,
   Who look for day before his mistress wakes.
Awake, awake, break through your veils of lawn!
Then draw your curtains, and begin the dawn.

SIR WILLIAM DAVENANT (1606–68)

The Thrush's Nest

Within a thick and spreading hawthorn bush
   That overhung a molehill large and round,
I heard from morn to morn a merry thrush
   Sing hymns to sunrise, and I drank the sound
With joy; and often, an intruding guest,
   I watched her secret toil from day to day.
How true she warped the moss, to form a nest,
   And modelled it within with wood and clay;
And by and by, like heath bells gilt with dew,
   There lay her shining eggs, as bright as flowers,
Ink-spotted-over shells of greeny blue;
   And there I witnessed in the sunny hours
A brood of nature's minstrels chirp and fly,
Glad as the sunshine and the laughing sky.

JOHN CLARE (1793–1864)

The Eagle

He clasps the crag with crooked hands;
Close to the sun in lonely lands,
Ringed with the azure world, he stands.
The wrinkled sea beneath him crawls;
He watches from his mountain walls,
And like a thunderbolt he falls.

ALFRED, LORD TENNYSON (1809–92)

Fish

Man's life is warm, glad, sad, 'twixt loves and graves,
Boundless in hope, honoured with pangs austere,
Heaven-gazing, and his angel-wings he craves;
The fish is swift, small-needing, vague yet clear,
A cold, sweet, silver life, wrapped in round waves,
Quickened with touches of transporting fear.

LEIGH HUNT (1784–1859)

La Fuite de la Lune

To outer senses there is peace,
A dreamy peace on either hand;
Deep silence in the shadowy land,
Deep silence where the shadows cease,

Save for a cry that echoes shrill
From some lone bird disconsolate,
A corncrake calling to its mate,
The answer from the misty hill.

And suddenly the moon withdraws
Her sickle from the lightening skies
And to her sombre cavern flies,
Wrapped in a veil of yellow gauze.

OSCAR WILDE (1854–1900)

This Blessèd Plot

Gaunt's Dying Speech

Methinks I am a prophet new inspir'd,
And thus expiring do foretell of him:
His rash fierce blaze of riot cannot last,
For violent fires soon burn out themselves;
Small showers last long, but sudden storms are short;
He tires betimes that spurs too fast betimes;
With eager feeding food doth choke the feeder:
Light vanity, insatiate cormorant,
Consuming means, soon preys upon itself.
This royal throne of kings, this scepter'd isle,
This earth of majesty, this seat of Mars,
This other Eden, demi-paradise,

This fortress built by Nature for herself
Against infection and the hand of war,
This happy breed of men, this little world,
This precious stone set in the silver sea,
Which serves it in the office of a wall,
Or as a moat defensive to a house,
Against the envy of less happier lands,
This blessèd plot, this earth, this realm, this England,
This nurse, this teeming womb of royal kings,
Fear'd by their breed and famous by their birth,
Renownèd for their deeds as far from home –
For Christian service and true chivalry –
As is the sepulchre in stubborn Jewry
Of the world's ransom, blessèd Mary's Son:
This land of such dear souls, this dear, dear land,
Dear for her reputation through the world,
Is now leas'd out – I die pronouncing it –
Like to a tenement, or pelting farm:
England, bound in with the triumphant sea
Whose rocky shore beats back the envious siege
Of watery Neptune, is now bound in with shame,

With inky blots, and rotten parchment bonds:
That England, that was wont to conquer others,
Hath made a shameful conquest of itself.
Ah! would the scandal vanish with my life,
How happy then were my ensuing death.

WILLIAM SHAKESPEARE (1564–1616), *Richard II*, 2, 1

The Air of England

Slaves cannot breathe in England; if their lungs
Receive our air, that moment they are free.
They touch our country and their shackles fall.

WILLIAM COWPER (1731–1800)

Home Thoughts from Abroad

Oh, to be in England
Now that April's there,

And whoever wakes in England
Sees, some morning, unaware,
That the lowest boughs and the brushwood sheaf
Round the elm-tree bole are in tiny leaf,
While the chaffinch sings on the orchard bough
In England – now!

And after April, when May follows,
And the whitethroat builds, and all the swallows –
Hark! where my blossomed pear tree in the hedge
Leans to the field and scatters on the clover
Blossoms and dewdrops – at the bent spray's edge –
That's the wise thrush; he sings each song twice over,
Lest you should think he never could recapture
The first fine careless rapture!
  And though the fields look rough with hoary dew,
  All will be gay when noontide wakes anew
  The buttercups, the little children's dower,
    – Far brighter than this gaudy melon-flower!

ROBERT BROWNING (1812–1889)

Love of England

England, with all thy faults, I love thee still,
My country! and while yet a nook is left
Where English minds and manners may be found,
Shall be constrain'd to love thee. Though thy clime
Be fickle, and thy year, most part deform'd
With dripping rains, or wither'd by a frost,
I would not yet exchange thy sullen skies
And fields without a flower for warmer France
With all her vines; nor for Ausonia's groves
Of golden fruitage and her myrtle bowers.
To shake thy senate, and from heights sublime
Of patriot eloquence to flash down fire
Upon thy foes, was never meant my task;
But I can feel thy fortunes, and partake
Thy joys and sorrows with as true a heart
As any thunderer there. And I can feel
Thy follies too, and with a just disdain
Frown at effeminates, whose very looks
Reflect dishonour on the land I love.

How, in the name of soldiership and sense,
Should England prosper, when such things, as smooth
And tender as a girl, all-essenced o'er
With odours, and as profligate as sweet,
Who sell their laurel for a myrtle wreath,
And love when they should fight; when such as these
Presume to lay their hand upon the ark
Of her magnificent and awful cause?
Time was when it was praise and boast enough
In every clime, and travel where we might,
That we were born her children; praise enough
To fill the ambition of a private man,
That Chatham's language was his mother-tongue,
And Wolfe's great name compatriot with his own.
Farewell those honours, and farewell with them
The hope of such hereafter. They have fallen
Each in his field of glory: one in arms,
And one in council – Wolfe upon the lap
Of smiling victory that moment won,
And Chatham, heart-sick of his country's shame!
They made us many soldiers. Chatham still

Consulting England's happiness at home,
Secured it by an unforgiving frown
If any wrong'd her. Wolfe, where'er he fought,
Put so much of his heart into his act,
That his example had a magnet's force,
And all were swift to follow whom all loved.
Those suns are set. Oh, rise some other such!
Or all that we have left is empty talk
Of old achievements and despair of new.

WILLIAM COWPER (1731–1800)

God's Residence

Who has not found the heaven below
    Will fail of it above.
God's residence is next to mine,
    His furniture is love.

EMILY DICKINSON (1880–86)

A Wish

Mine be a cot beside the hill;
   A beehive's hum shall soothe my ear;
A willowy brook, that turns a mill,
   With many a fall shall linger near.

The swallow oft beneath my thatch
   Shall twitter from her clay-built nest;
Oft shall the pilgrim lift the latch
   And share my meal, a welcome guest.

Around my ivied porch shall spring
   Each fragrant flower that drinks the dew;
And Lucy at her wheel shall sing
   In russet gown and apron blue.

The village church among the trees,
   Where first our marriage vows were given,
With merry peals shall swell the breeze
   And point with taper spire to heaven.

SAMUEL ROGERS (1763–1855)

A Vanished Village

Is this the ground where generations lie
  Mourn'd by the drooping birch and dewy fern,
  And by the faithful, alder-shaded burn,

Which seems to breathe an everlasting sigh?
No sign of habitation meets the eye;
  Only some ancient furrows I discern,
  And verdant mounds, and from them sadly learn

That hereabout men used to live and die.
Once the blue vapour of the smouldering peat
  From half a hundred homes would curl on high,
While round the doors rang children's voices sweet;
  Where now the timid deer goes wandering by,
Or a lost lamb sends forth a plaintive bleat,
  And the lone glen looks up to the lone sky.

R. WILTON

I Vow to Thee, My Country

I vow to thee, my country – all earthly things above –
Entire and whole and perfect, the service of my love,
The love that asks no question, the love that
                                        stands the test,
That lays upon the altar the dearest and the best;
The love that never falters, the love that pays the price,
The love that makes undaunted the final sacrifice.

And there's another country, I've heard of long ago –
Most dear to them that love her, most great to
                                        them that know –
We may not count her armies; we may not see
                                        her king –
Her fortress is a faithful heart, her pride is suffering –
And soul by soul and silently her shining bounds
                                        increase
And her ways are ways of gentleness and all her
                                        paths are peace.

SIR CECIL SPRING-RICE (1859–1918)

184

Jerusalem

And did those feet in ancient time
Walk upon England's mountains green?
And was the holy Lamb of God
On England's pleasant pastures seen?

And did the Countenance Divine
Shine forth upon our clouded hills?
And was Jerusalem builded here
Among these dark satanic mills?

Bring me my bow of burning gold!
Bring me my arrows of desire!
Bring me my spear! O clouds, unfold!
Bring me my chariot of fire!

I will not cease from mental fight,
Nor shall my sword sleep in my hand,
Till we have built Jerusalem
In England's green and pleasant land.

WILLIAM BLAKE (1757–1827)

The Banks o' Doon

Ye banks and braes o' bonie Doon,
    How can ye bloom sae fresh and fair;
How can ye chant, ye little birds,
    And I sae weary, fu' o' care!
Thou'll break my heart, thou warbling bird,
    That wantons through the flowering thorn:
Thou minds me o' departed joys,
    Departed, never to return.

Oft hae I roved by bonnie Doon,
    To see the rose and woodbine twine;
And ilka bird sang o' its luve,
    And fondly sae did I o' mine.
Wi' lightsome heart I pu'd a rose,
    Fu' sweet upon its thorny tree;
And my fause luver staw my rose,
    But, ah! he left the thorn wi' me.

ROBERT BURNS (1759–96)

Impression de Voyage

The sea was sapphire coloured, and the sky
  Burned like a heated opal through the air;
  We hoisted sail; the wind was blowing fair
For the blue lands that to the eastward lie.
From the steep prow I marked with quickening eye
  Zakynthos, every olive grove and creek,
  Ithaca's cliff, Lycaon's snowy peak,
And all the flower-strewn hills of Arcady.
The flapping of the sail against the mast,
  The ripple of the water on the side,
  The ripple of girls' laughter at the stern,
The only sounds: – when 'gan the west to burn,
  And a red sun upon the seas to ride,
  I stood upon the soil of Greece at last!

OSCAR WILDE (1854–1900)

Tall Nettles

Tall nettles cover up, as they have done
These many springs, the rusty harrow, the plough
Long worn out, and the roller made of stone:
Only the elm butt tops the nettles now.

This corner of the farmyard I like most:
As well as any bloom upon a flower
I like the dust on the nettles, never lost
Except to prove the sweetness of a shower.

EDWARD THOMAS (1878–1917)

Boston

I come from the city of Boston,
The home of the bean and the cod,
Where Cabots speak only to Lowells,
And Lowells speak only to God.

SAMUEL C. BUSHNELL

Composed upon Westminster Bridge

Earth has not anything to show more fair:
Dull would he be of soul who could pass by
A sight so touching in its majesty:
This city now doth like a garment wear
The beauty of the morning; silent, bare,
Ships, towers, domes, theatres, and temples lie
Open unto the fields, and to the sky;
All bright and glittering in the smokeless air.
Never did sun more beautifully steep
In his first splendour, valley, rock, or hill;
Ne'er saw I, never felt, a calm so deep!
The river glideth at his own sweet will:
Dear God! the very houses seem asleep;
And all that mighty heart is lying still!

WILLIAM WORDSWORTH (1770–1850)

Goodly London

O more than mortall man, that did this towne begin!
Whose knowledge found the plot, so fit to set it in.
What God, or heavenly power was harbourd in thy breast,
From whom with such successe thy labours should

be blest?
Built on a rising bank, within a vale to stand,
And for thy healthfull soyle, chose gravell mixt

with sand . . .
And to the north and south, upon an equall reach,
Two hills their even banks do somewhat seeme to stretch,
Those two extreamer winds from hurting it to let;
And only levell lies, upon the rise and set.
Of all this goodly ile, where breathes most cheerefull aire,
And every way thereto the wayes most smooth and faire;
As in the fittest place, by man that could be thought,
To which by land, or sea, provision might be brought.
And such a road for ships scarce all the world commands,
As is the goodly Thames, neer where Brute's City stands.

Nor any haven lies to which is more resort,
Commodities to bring, as also to transport.

MICHAEL DRAYTON (1563–1631)

In London

Here malice, rapine, accident conspire,
And now a rabble rages, now a fire;
Their ambush here relentless ruffians lay,
And here the fell attorney prowls for prey;
Here falling houses thunder on your head,
And here a female atheist talks you dead.

DR SAMUEL JOHNSON (1709–84)

London

I wander thro' each charter'd street,
Near where the charter'd Thames does flow,
And mark in every face I meet
Marks of weakness, marks of woe.

In every cry of every Man,
In every Infant's cry of fear,
In every voice, in every ban,
The mind-forg'd manacles I hear.

How the chimney-sweeper's cry
Every black'ning church appals;
And the hapless soldier's sigh
Runs in blood down palace walls.

But most thro' midnight streets I hear
How the youthful harlot's curse
Blasts the new-born infant's tear,
And blights with plagues the marriage hearse.

WILLIAM BLAKE (1757–1827)

That Great Sea

London: that great sea whose ebb and flow
At once is deaf and loud, and on the shore
Vomits its wrecks, and still howls on for more.
Yet in its depths what treasures!

PERCY BYSHE SHELLEY (1792–1822)

London

A mighty mass of brick and smoke and shipping,
Dirty and dusky, but as wide as eye
Could reach, with here and there a sail just skipping
In sight, then lost amidst the forestry
Of masts: a wilderness of steeples peeping
On tip-toe through their sea coal canopy:
A huge dun cupola like a foolscap crown
On a fool's head – and there is London Town.

GEORGE GORDON, LORD BYRON (1788–1824)

London Snow

When men were all asleep the snow came flying,
In large white flakes falling on the city brown,
Stealthily and perpetually settling and loosely lying,
    Hushing the latest traffic of the drowsy town;
Deadening, muffling, stifling its murmurs failing;
Lazily and incessantly floating down and down:
    Silently sifting and veiling road, roof and railing;
Hiding difference, making unevenness even,
Into angles and crevices softly drifting and sailing.
    All night it fell, and when full inches seven
It lay in the depth of its uncompacted lightness,
The clouds blew off from a high and frosty heaven;
    And all woke earlier for the unaccustomed brightness
Of the winter dawning, the strange unheavenly glare:
The eye marvelled – marvelled at the dazzling whiteness;
    The ear hearkened to the stillness of the solemn air;
No sound of wheel rumbling nor of foot falling,
And the busy morning cries came thin and spare.
    Then boys I heard, as they went to school, calling,

They gathered up the crystal manna to freeze
Their tongues with tasting, their hands with snowballing;
    Or rioted in a drift, plunging up to the knees;
Or peering up from under the white-mossed wonder,
'O look at the trees!' they cried. 'O look at the trees!'

    With lessened load, a few carts creak and blunder,
Following along the white deserted way,
A country company long dispersed asunder:
    When now already the sun, in pale display
Standing by Paul's high dome, spread forth below
His sparkling beams, and awoke the stir of the day.

    For now doors open, and war is waged with the snow;
And trains of sombre men, past tale of number,
Tread long brown paths, as toward their toil they go:
    But even for them awhile no cares encumber
Their minds diverted; the daily word is unspoken,
The daily thoughts of labour and sorrow slumber
At the sight of the beauty that greets them, for the
                              charm they have broken.

ROBERT BRIDGES (1844–1930)

London

Athwart the sky, a lowly sigh
From west to east the sweet wind carried;
The sun stood still on Primrose Hill;
   His light in all the city tarried:
The clouds on viewless columns bloomed
Like smouldering lilies unconsumed.

'Oh sweetheart, see! how shadowy,
   Of some occult magician's rearing,
Or swung in space of heaven's grace
   Dissolving, dimly reappearing,
Afloat upon ethereal tides
St Paul's above the city rides!'

A rumour broke through the thin smoke
   Enwreathing abbey, tower, and palace,
The parks, the squares, the thoroughfares,
   The million-peopled lanes and alleys,
An ever-muttering prisoned storm,
The heart of London beating warm.

JOHN DAVIDSON (1857–1909)

Symphony in Yellow

An omnibus across the bridge
   Crawls like a yellow butterfly,
    And, here and there, a passer-by
Shows like a little restless midge.

Big barges full of yellow hay
   Are moved against the shadowy wharf,
    And, like a yellow silken scarf,
The thick fog hangs along the quay.

The yellow leaves begin to fade
   And flutter from the Temple elms,
    And at my feet the pale green Thames
Lies like a rod of rippled jade.

OSCAR WILDE (1854–1900)

Manhattan

City of orgies, walks and joys,
City whom I that have lived and sung in your midst
    will one day make you illustrious,
Not the pageants of you, not your shifting tableaux,
    your spectacles, repay me,
Not the interminable rows of your houses, nor the
    ships at the wharves,
Nor the processions in the street, nor the bright
    windows with goods in them,
Nor to converse with learn'd persons, or bear my share
    in the soirée or feast;
Not those, but as I pass, O Manhattan, your frequent
    and swift flash of eyes offering me love,
Offering response to my own – these repay me,
Lovers, continual lovers, only repay me.

WALT WHITMAN (1819–91)

In Time of 'The Breaking of Nations'

Only a man harrowing clods
　　In a slow silent walk
With an old horse that stumbles and nods
　　Half asleep as they stalk.

Only thin smoke without flame
　　From the heaps of couch-grass;
Yet this will go onward the same
　　Though dynasties pass.

Yonder a maid and her wight
　　Come whispering by:
War's annals will cloud into night
　　Ere their story die.

THOMAS HARDY (1840–1928)

Adlestrop

Yes. I remember Adlestrop –
The name, because one afternoon
Of heat the express-train drew up there
Unwontedly. It was late June.

The steam hissed. Someone cleared his throat.
No one left and no one came
On the bare platform. What I saw
Was Adlestrop – only the name –

And willows, willow-herb, and grass,
And meadowsweet, and haycocks dry,
No whit less still and lonely fair
Than the high cloudlets in the sky.

And for that minute a blackbird sang
Close by, and round him, mistier,
Farther and farther, all the birds
Of Oxfordshire and Gloucestershire.

EDWARD THOMAS (1878–1917)

The Business of Love

An Appeal to Cats in the Business of Love

Ye cats that at midnight spit love at each other,
Who best feel the pangs of a passionate lover,
I appeal to your scratches and your tattered fur,
If the business of love be no more than to purr.
Old Lady Grimalkin with her gooseberry eyes,
Knew something when a kitten, for why she was wise;
You find by experience, the love-fit's soon o'er,
Puss! Puss! lasts not long, but turns to *Cat-whore!*

      Men ride many miles,
      Cats tread many tiles,
    Both hazard their necks in the fray;
      Only cats, when they fall
      From a house or a wall,
  Keep their feet, mount their tails, and away.

THOMAS FLATMAN (1637–88)

Eternity

He who bends to himself a joy
Doth the wingèd life destroy;
But he who kisses the joy as it flies
Lives in eternity's sunrise.

WILLIAM BLAKE (1757–1827)

To His Coy Mistress

Had we but world enough, and time,
This coyness, lady, were no crime.
We would sit down, and think which way
To walk, and pass our long love's day.
Thou by the Indian Ganges' side
Should'st rubies find: I by the tide
Of Humber would complain. I would

Love you ten years before the Flood,
And you should, if you please, refuse
Till the conversion of the Jews.
My vegetable love should grow
Vaster than empires and more slow;
An hundred years should go to praise
Thine eyes, and on thy forehead gaze;
Two hundred to adore each breast,
But thirty thousand to the rest;
An age at least to every part,
And the last age should show your heart.
For, lady, you deserve this state,
Nor would I love at lower rate.
  But at my back I always hear
Time's wingèd chariot hurrying near,
And yonder all before us lie
Deserts of vast eternity.
Thy beauty shall no more be found,
Nor, in thy marble vault, shall sound
My echoing song; then worms shall try

That long-preserved virginity,
And your quaint honour turn to dust,
And into ashes all my lust:
The grave's a fine and private place,
But none, I think, do there embrace.
  Now therefore, while the youthful hue
Sits on thy skin like morning dew,
And while thy willing soul transpires
At every pore with instant fires,
Now let us sport us while we may,
And now, like amorous birds of prey,
Rather at once our time devour
Than languish in his slow-chapt power.
Let us roll all our strength and all
Our sweetness up into one ball,
And tear our pleasures with rough strife,
Thorough the iron gates of life;
Thus, though we cannot make our sun
Stand still, yet we will make him run.

ANDREW MARVELL (1621–78)

Goodnight

Bid me no more goodnight; because
   'Tis dark, must I away?
Love doth acknowledge no such laws,
   And love 'tis I obey;
Which blind, doth all your light despise,
   And hath no need of eyes
     When day is fled.
   Besides, the sun, which you
   Complain is gone, 'tis true,
    Is gone to bed:
   Oh, let us do so too.

JAMES SHIRLEY (1596–1666)

The Sun Rising

     Busy old fool, unruly Sun,
       Why dost thou thus,
Through windows, and through curtains call on us?
Must to thy motions lovers' seasons run?
     Saucy pedantic wretch, go chide
     Late schoolboys and sour 'prentices,
  Go tell court-huntsmen that the king will ride,
  Call country ants to harvest offices;
Love, all alike, no season knows, nor clime,
Nor hours, days, months, which are the rags of time.

     Thy beams so reverend, and strong
       Why shouldst thou think?
I could eclipse and cloud them with a wink,
But that I would not lose her sight so long:
     If her eyes have not blinded thine,
     Look, and tomorrow late, tell me,
    Whether both the Indias of spice and mine

Be where thou left'st them, or lie here with me.
Ask for those kings whom thou saw'st yesterday,
And thou shalt hear, 'All here in one bed lay.'

      She's all states, and all princes I,
        Nothing else is.
Princes do but play us; compared to this,
All honour's mimic; all wealth alchemy.
      Thou, Sun, art half as happy as we,
        In that the world's contracted thus;
   Thine age asks ease, and since thy duties be
   To warm the world, that's done in warming us.
Shine here to us, and thou art everywhere;
This bed thy centre is, these walls thy sphere.

JOHN DONNE (1572–1631)

Let Me Not to the Marriage of True Minds

Let me not to the marriage of true minds
Admit impediments. Love is not love
Which alters when it alteration finds,
Or bends with the remover to remove.
O, no! it is an ever-fixèd mark,
That looks on tempests and is never shaken;
It is the star to every wandering bark,
Whose worth's unknown, although his height be taken.
Love's not Time's fool, though rosy lips and cheeks
Within his bending sickle's compass come;
Love alters not with his brief hours and weeks,
But bears it out even to the edge of doom.
  If this be error, and upon me proved,
  I never writ, nor no man ever loved.

WILLIAM SHAKESPEARE (1564–1616)

Absence

Absence, hear thou this protestation
   Against thy strength,
   Distance, and length;
Do what thou canst for alteration:
   For hearts of truest mettle
Absence doth join, and time doth settle.

Who loves a mistress of such quality,
   His mind hath found
   Affection's ground
Beyond time, place, and mortality.
   To hearts that cannot vary
Absence is present, time doth tarry.

My senses want their outward motion
   Which now within
   Reason doth win,
Redoubled by her secret notion:
   Like rich men that take pleasure
In hiding more than handling treasure.

By absence this good means I gain,
   That I can catch her,
   Where none can match her,
In some close corner of my brain;
   There I embrace and kiss her:
And so I both enjoy and miss her.

JOHN DONNE (1572–1631)

To Electra

I dare not ask a kiss;
   I dare not beg a smile;
Lest having that, or this,
   I might grow proud the while.

No, no, the utmost share
   Of my desire shall be
Only to kiss that air
   That lately kissed thee.

ROBERT HERRICK (1591–1674)

There is Lady Sweet and Kind

There is a lady sweet and kind,
Was never face so pleased my mind;
I did but see her passing by,
And yet I love her till I die.

Her gesture, motion, and her smiles,
Her wit, her voice, my heart beguiles,
Beguiles my heart, I know not why,
And yet I love her till I die.

Cupid is wingèd and doth range,
Her country so my love doth change:
But change she earth, or change she sky,
Yet will I love her till I die.

ANONYMOUS

Shall I Compare Thee to a Summer's Day?

Shall I compare thee to a summer's day?
Thou art more lovely and more temperate:
Rough winds do shake the darling buds of May,
And summer's lease hath all too short a date:
Sometime too hot the eye of heaven shines,
And often is his gold complexion dimm'd;
And every fair from fair sometime declines,
By chance or nature's changing course untrimm'd;
But thy eternal summer shall not fade,
Nor lose possession of that fair thou ow'st,
Nor shall death brag thou wander'st in his shade,
When in eternal lines to time thou grow'st;
   So long as men can breathe, or eyes can see,
   So long lives this, and this gives life to thee.

WILLIAM SHAKESPEARE (1564–1616)

My True Love Hath My Heart

My true love hath my heart, and I have his,
By just exchange one for the other given.
I hold his dear, and mine he cannot miss:
There never was a better bargain driven.
His heart in me keeps me and him in one;
My heart in him his thoughts and senses guides;
He loves my heart, for once it was his own;
I cherish his, because in me it bides.
His heart his wound receivèd from my sight;
My heart was wounded with his wounded heart;
For as from me on him his hurt did light;
So still, methought, in me his hurt did smart;
    Both equal hurt, in this change sought our bliss:
    My true love hath my heart, and I have his.

SIR PHILIP SIDNEY (1554–86)

Love's Reckoning

How do I love thee? Let me count the ways.
I love thee to the depth and breadth and height
My soul can reach, when feeling out of sight
For the ends of Being and ideal Grace.
I love thee to the level of every day's
Most quiet need, by sun and candlelight.
I love thee freely, as men strive for Right;
I love thee purely, as they turn from Praise;
I love thee with the passion put to use
In my old griefs, and with my childhood's faith.
I love thee with a love I seemed to lose
With my lost saints – I love thee with the breath,
Smiles, tears, of all my life! – and, if God choose,
I shall but love thee better after death.

ELIZABETH BARRETT BROWNING (1809–61)

When in the Chronicle of Wasted Time

When in the chronicle of wasted time
I see descriptions of the fairest wights,
And beauty making beautiful old rhyme,
In praise of ladies dead, and lovely knights,
Then in the blazon of sweet beauty's best,
Of hand, of foot, of lip, of eye, of brow,
I see their antique pen would have express'd
Even such a beauty as you master now.
So all their praises are but prophecies
Of this our time, all you prefiguring;
And, for they look'd but with divining eyes,
They had not skill enough your worth to sing:
    For we, which now behold these present days,
    Have eyes to wonder but lack tongues to praise.

WILLIAM SHAKESPEARE (1564–1616)

Is She Not Pure Gold

Nay, but you, who do not love her,
   Is she not pure gold, my mistress?
Holds earth aught – speak truth – above her?
   Aught like this tress, see, and this tress,
And this last fairest tress of all,
So fair, see, ere I let it fall?

Because you spend your lives in praising:
   To praise you search the wide world over:
Then why not witness, calmly gazing,
   If earth holds aught – speak truth – above her?
Above this tress, and this, I touch
But cannot praise, I love so much.

ROBERT BROWNING (1812–89)

The Power of Love

When in disgrace with fortune and men's eyes,
I all alone beweep my outcast state,
And trouble deaf Heaven with my bootless cries,
And look upon myself, and curse my fate,
Wishing me like to one more rich in hope,
Featur'd like him, like him with friends possess'd,
Desiring this man's art, and that man's scope,
With what I most enjoy contented least;
Yet in these thoughts myself almost despising,
Haply I think on thee – and then my state
(Like to the lark at break of day arising
From sullen earth) sings hymns at heaven's gate;
   For thy sweet love remember'd such wealth brings,
   That then I scorn to change my state with kings.

WILLIAM SHAKESPEARE (1564–1616)

Worth Dying For

If we shall live, we live:
If we shall die, we die:
If we live, we shall meet again:
But tonight, goodbye.
One word, let but one be heard –
What not one word?

If we sleep, we shall wake again
And see tomorrow's light:
If we wake, we shall meet again:
But tonight, good-night.
Good-night, my lost and found –
Still not a sound?

If we live, we must part;
If we die, we part in pain:
If we die, we shall part
Only to meet again.

By those tears on either cheek,
Tomorrow you will speak.

To meet, worth living for:
Worth dying for, to meet,
To meet, worth parting for:
Bitter forgot in sweet
To meet, worth parting before,
Never to part more.

CHRISTINA ROSSETTI (1830–94)

Love

Love is anterior to life,
    Posterior to death,
Initial of creation and
    The exponent of breath.

EMILY DICKINSON (1830–86)

Now Sleeps the Crimson Petal

Now sleeps the crimson petal, now the white;
Nor waves the cypress in the palace walk;
Nor winks the gold fin in the porphyry font:
The firefly wakens: waken thou with me.

Now droops the milk-white peacock like a ghost,
And like a ghost she glimmers on to me.

Now lies the earth all Danaë to the stars,
And all thy heart lies open unto me.

Now slides the silent meteor on, and leaves
A shining furrow, as thy thoughts in me.

Now folds the lily all her sweetness up,
And slips into the bosom of the lake:
So fold thyself, my dearest, thou, and slip
Into my bosom and be lost in me.

ALFRED, LORD TENNYSON (1809–92)

Love is Enough

Love is enough: though the world be a-waning,
And the woods have no voice but the voice of
                                    complaining,
Though the skies be too dark for dim eyes to discover
The gold-cups and daisies fair blooming thereunder,
Though the hills be held shadows, and the sea a
                                    dark wonder,
And this day draw a veil over all deeds passed over,
Yet their hands shall not tremble, their feet shall
                                    not falter:
The void shall not weary, the fear shall not alter
These lips and these eyes of the loved and the lover.

WILLIAM MORRIS (1834–96)

A Red, Red Rose

O my luve's like a red, red rose,
   That's newly sprung in June;
O my luve's like the melodie
   That's sweetly played in tune.

As fair art thou, my bonnie lass,
   So deep in luve am I;
And I will love thee still, my dear,
   Till a' the seas gang dry.

Till a' the seas gang dry, my dear,
   And the rocks melt wi' the sun:
I will love thee still, my dear,
   While the sands o' life shall run.

And fare thee weel, my only luve!
   And fare thee weel, a while!
And I will come again, my luve,
   Though it were ten thousand mile!

ROBERT BURNS (1759–96)

To Celia

Drink to me only with thine eyes,
    And I will pledge with mine;
Or leave a kiss but in the cup
    And I'll not look for wine.
The thirst that from the soul doth rise
    Doth ask a drink divine;
But might I of Jove's nectar sup,
    I would not change for thine.

I sent thee late a rosy wreath,
    Not so much honouring thee
As giving it a hope that there
    It could not wither'd be;
But thou thereon didst only breathe
    And sent'st it back to me;
Since when it grows, and smells, I swear,
    Not of itself but thee!

BEN JONSON (1572–1637)

Love and Life

All my past life is mine no more,
　　The flying hours are gone:
Like transitory dreams giv'n o'er,
Whose images are kept in store,
　　By memory alone.

The time that is to come is not;
　　How can it then be mine?
The present moment's all my lot;
And that, as fast as it is got,
　　Phillis, is only thine.

Then talk not of inconstancy,
　　False hearts, and broken vows;
If I, by miracle, can be
This live-long minute true to thee,
　　'Tis all that Heav'n allows.

JOHN WILMOT, EARL OF ROCHESTER (1647–80)

She Walks in Beauty

She walks in beauty, like the night
   Of cloudless climes and starry skies;
And all that's best of dark and bright
   Meet in her aspect and her eyes:
Thus mellowed to that tender light
   Which heaven to gaudy day denies.

One shade the more, one ray the less,
   Had half impaired the nameless grace,
Which waves in every raven tress,
   Or softly lightens o'er her face;
Where thoughts serenely sweet express,
   How pure, how dear their dwelling-place.

And on the cheek, and o'er that brow,
   So soft, so calm, yet eloquent,
The smiles that win, the tints that glow,
   But tell of days in goodness spent,
A mind at peace with all below,
   A heart whose love is innocent!

GEORGE GORDON, LORD BYRON (1788–1824)

The Church Porch

Although I enter not,
Yet round about the spot
   Sometimes I hover:
And at the sacred gate,
With longing eyes I wait,
   Expectant of her.

The minster bell tolls out
Above the city's rout
   And noise and humming:
They've stopped the chiming bell:
I hear the organ's swell:
   She's coming – coming!

My lady comes at last,
Timid, and stepping fast,
   And hastening hither,
With modest eyes downcast:

She comes – she's here – she's past –
   May heaven go with her!

Kneel, undisturb'd, fair saint!
Pour out your praise or plaint
   Meekly and duly;
I will not enter there,
To sully your pure prayer
   With thoughts unruly.

But suffer me to pace
Round the forbidden place,
   Lingering a minute,
Like outcast spirits who wait
And see through Heaven's gate
   Angels within it.

WILLIAM MAKEPEACE THACKERAY (1811–63)

227

A Song of a Young Lady to her Ancient Lover

Ancient person, for whom I
All the flattering youth defy,
Long be it ere thou grow old,
Aching, shaking, crazy, cold,
But still continue as thou art
Ancient person of my heart.

On thy withered lips and dry,
Which like barren furrows lie,
Brooding kisses I will pour
Shall thy youthful heat restore.
Such kind showers in autumn fall,
And a second spring recall,
Nor from thee will ever part,
Ancient person of my heart.

Thy nobler part, which but to name
In our sex would be counted shame,
By age's frozen grasp possessed,

From his ice shall be released,
And, soothed by my reviving hand,
In former warmth and vigour stand.
All a lover's wish can reach,
For thy joy my love shall teach,
And for thy pleasure shall improve
All that art can add to love.
Yet still I love thee without art,
Ancient person of my heart

JOHN WILMOT, EARL OF ROCHESTER
(1648–80)

To a Woman

Since all that I can do for thee
Is to do nothing, this my prayer must be;
That thou may'st never guess nor ever see
The all-endured this nothing-done costs me.

LORD LYTTON (1803–73)

Love Me Not for Comely Grace

Love not me for comely grace,
    For my pleasing eye or face,
Nor for any outward part,
No, nor for my constant heart –
    For those may fail, or turn to ill,
        So thou and I shall sever:
Keep therefore a true woman's eye,
And love me still, but know not why –
    So hast thou the same reason still
        To doat upon me ever!

ANONYMOUS

If Thou Must Love Me

If thou must love me, let it be for nought
Except for love's sake only. Do not say,
'I love her for her smile. . . her look. . . her way
Of speaking gently . . . for a trick of thought
That falls in well with mine, and certes brought
A sense of pleasant ease on such a day –
For these things in themselves, Belovèd, may
Be changed, or change for thee – and love so wrought,
May be unwrought so. Neither love me for
Thine own dear pity's wiping my cheeks dry,
Since one might well forget to weep who bore
Thy comfort long, and lose thy love thereby.
But love me for love's sake, that evermore
Thou may'st love on through love's eternity.

ELIZABETH BARRETT BROWNING (1806–61)

The Taxi

When I go away from you
The world beats dead,
Like a slackened drum.
I call out for you against the jutted stars
And shout into the ridges of the wind.

Streets coming fast,
One after the other,
Wedge you away from me,
And the lamps of the city prick my eyes
So that I can no longer see your face.
Why should I leave you,
To wound myself upon the sharp
                          edges of the night?

AMY LOWELL (1874–1925)

If You Were Coming

If you were coming in the fall,
I'd brush the summer by
With half a smile and half a spurn,
As housewives do a fly.

EMILY DICKINSON (1830–86)

Unhappy Love

I see she flies me everywhere,
Her eyes her scorn discover;
   But what's her scorn, or my despair,
   Since 'tis my fate to love her?
Were she but kind, whom I adore,
I might live longer, but not love her more.

ANONYMOUS

Renouncement

I must not think of thee; and, tired yet strong,
I shun the thought that lurks in all delight –
The thought of thee – and in the blue heaven's height,
And in the sweetest passage of a song.
Oh just beyond the fairest thoughts that throng
This breast, the thought of thee waits hidden yet bright;
But it must never, never come in sight;
I must stop short of thee the whole day long.
But when sleep comes to close each difficult day,
When night gives pause to the long watch I keep,
And all my bonds I needs must loose apart,
Must doff my will as raiment laid away –
   With the first dream that comes with the first sleep,
   I run, I run, I am gathered to thy heart.

ALICE MEYNELL (1847–1922)

Echo

Come to me in the silence of the night:
   Come in the speaking silence of a dream;
Come with soft rounded cheeks and eyes as bright
   As sunlight on a stream;
     Come back in tears,
O memory, hope, love of finished years.

O dream how sweet, too sweet, too bitter sweet,
   Whose wakening should have been in Paradise,
Where souls brimful of love abide and meet;
   Where thirsting, longing eyes
     Watch the slow door
That opening, letting in, lets out no more.

Yet come to me in dreams, that I may live
   My very life again though cold in death:
Come back to me in dreams, that I may give
   Pulse for pulse, breath for breath:

Speak low, lean low,
As long ago, my love, how long ago!

CHRISTINA ROSSETTI (1830–94)

If You Love Me, Don't Pursue Me

Get you gone, you will undo me!
If you love me, don't pursue me;
Let that inclination perish
Which I dare no longer cherish;
At ev'ry hour, in ev'ry place,
I either see or form your face;
My dreams at night are all of you!
Such as till now I never knew:
I've sported thus with young desire,
Never intending to go higher.
You found me harmless; leave me so;
For were I not – you'd leave me too.

SIR CHARLES SEDLEY (c.1639–1701)

To F—

Beloved! amid the earnest woes
   That crowd around my earthly path –
(Drear path, alas! where grows
Not even one lonely rose) –
   My soul at least a solace hath
In dreams of thee, and therein knows
An Eden of bland repose.

And thus thy memory is to me
   Like some enchanted far-off isle
In some tumultuous sea –
Some ocean throbbing far and free
   With storm – but where meanwhile
Serenest skies continually
   Just o'er that one bright island smile.

EDGAR ALLAN POE (1809–49)

The Reconcilement

Come, let us now resolve at last
To live and love in quiet;
We'll tie the knot so very fast
That time shall ne'er untie it.

The truest joys they seldom prove
Who free from quarrels live:
'Tis the most tender part of love
Each other to forgive.

When least I seemed concerned, I took
No pleasure, nor no rest;
And when I feigned an angry look,
Alas! I loved you best.

Own but the same to me – you'll find
How blest will be our fate.
O to be happy – to be kind
Sure never is too late!

JOHN SHEFFIELD, DUKE OF BUCKINGHAM (1648–1721)

To the Ladies

Wife and servant are the same,
But only differ in the name:
For when that fatal knot is tied,
Which nothing, nothing can divide,
When she the word *obey* has said,
And man by law supreme has made,
Then all that's kind is laid aside,
And nothing left but state and pride.
Fierce as an eastern prince he grows,
And all his innate rigour shows:
Then but to look, to laugh, or speak,
Will the nuptial contract break.
Like mutes, she signs alone must make,
And never any freedom take,
But still be governed by a nod,
And fear her husband as her god:
Him still must serve, him still obey,
And nothing act, and nothing say,

But what her haughty lord thinks fit,
Who, with the power, has all the wit.
Then shun, oh! shun that wretched state,
And all the fawning flatt'rers hate.
Value yourselves, and men despise:
You must be proud, if you'll be wise.

LADY MARY CHUDLEIGH (1656–1710)

On Marriage

How happy a thing were a wedding,
And a bedding,
If a man might purchase a wife
For a twelvemonth and a day;
But to live with her all a man's life,
For ever and for aye,
Till she grow as grey as a cat,
Good faith, Mr Parson, I thank you for that!

THOMAS FLATMAN (1637–88)

Advice to Her Son on Marriage

When you gain her affection, take care to preserve it;
Lest others persuade her, you do not deserve it.
Still study to heighten the joys of her life;
Not treat her the worse, for her being your wife.
If in judgement she errs, set her right, without pride:
'Tis the province of insolent fools to deride.
A husband's first praise is a friend and protector:
Then change not these titles for tyrant and hector.
Let your person be neat, unaffectedly clean,
Tho' alone with your wife the whole day you remain.
Choose books for her study to fashion her mind,
To emulate those who excelled of her kind.
Be religion the principal care of your life,
As you hope to be blest in your children and wife;
So you, in your marriage, shall gain its true end;
And find, in your wife, a companion and friend.

MARY BARBER (c.1690–1757)

Love is a Sickness

Love is a sickness full of woes,
   All remedies refusing:
A plant that with most cutting grows,
   Most barren with best using.
                  Why so?
More we enjoy it, more it dies,
If not enjoy'd, it sighing cries,
                  Hey ho.

Love is a torment of the mind,
   A tempest everlasting;
And Jove hath made it of a kind,
   Not well, nor full, nor fasting.
                  Why so?
More we enjoy it, more it dies,
If not enjoy'd, it sighing cries,
                  Hey ho.

SAMUEL DANIEL (1562–1619)

Love Shortens Tedious Nights

Now winter nights enlarge
  The number of their hours,
And clouds their storms discharge
  Upon the airy towers.
Let now the chimneys blaze
  And cups o'erflow with wine;
Let well-tuned words amaze
  With harmony divine.
Now yellow waxen lights
  Shall wait on honey love,
While youthful revels, masques, and
                    courtly sights
  Sleep's leaden spells remove.

This time doth well dispense
  With lovers' long discourse:
Much speech hath some defence,
  Though beauty no remorse.

All do not all things well:
    Some measures comely tread,
Some knotted riddles tell,
    Some poems smoothly read.
The summer hath his joys,
    And winter his delights.
Though love and all his pleasures are but toys,
    They shorten tedious nights.

THOMAS CAMPION (1567–1620)

The Question Answered

What is it men in women do require?
The lineaments of gratified desire.
What is it women do in men require?
The lineaments of gratified desire.

WILLIAM BLAKE (1757–1827)

A Sudden Light

I have been here before,
    But when or how I cannot tell:
I know the grass beyond the door,
    The sweet keen smell,
The sighing sound, the lights around the shore.

You have been mine before –
    How long ago I may not know:
But just when at that swallow's soar
    Your neck turned so,
Some veil did fall – I knew it all of yore.

Has this been thus before?
    And shall not thus time's eddying flight
Still with our lives our love restore
    In death's despite,
And day and night yield one delight once more?

DANTE GABRIEL ROSSETTI (1828–82)

Elegy

He or she that hopes to gain
Love's best sweet without some pain,
Hopes in vain.

Cupid's livery no one wears
But must put on hopes and fears,
Smiles and tears,

And, like to April weather,
Rain and shine both together,
Both or neither.

ANONYMOUS

Her Name is at My Tongue

Her name is at my tongue whene'er I speak,
Her shape's before my eyes where'er I stir,
Both day and night, as if her ghost did walk
And not she me but I had murdered her.

PHILIP AYRES (1638–1712)

The Clod and the Pebble

'Love seeketh not itself to please,
Nor for itself hath any care,
But for another gives its ease,
And builds a Heaven in Hell's despair.'

So sung a little Clod of clay,
Trodden with the cattle's feet,
But a Pebble of the brook
Warbled out these metres meet:

'Love seeketh only self to please,
To bind another to its delight,
Joys in another's loss of ease,
And builds a Hell in Heaven's despite.'

WILLIAM BLAKE (1757–1827)

The Divorce

Dear, back my wounded heart restore,
And turn away thy powerful eyes;
Flatter my willing soul no more!
Love must not hope what fate denies.

Take, take away thy smiles and kisses!
Thy love wounds deeper than disdain,
For he that sees the heaven he misses
Sustains two hells – of loss and pain . . .

THOMAS STANLEY (1625–78)

The Lady Who Offers
Her Looking-Glass to Venus

Venus, take my votive glass;
    Since I am not what I was.
What from this day I shall be,
    Venus, let me never see.

MATTHEW PRIOR (1664–1721)

Since There's No Help,
Come Let Us Kiss and Part

Since there's no help, come let us kiss and part.
Nay, I have done; you get no more of me,
And I am glad, yea, glad with all my heart,
That thus so cleanly I myself can free;
Shake hands for ever, cancel all our vows.
And when we meet at any time again,
Be it not seen in either of our brows
That we one jot of former love retain.
Now at the last gasp of Love's latest breath,
When, his pulse failing, Passion speechless lies,
When Faith is kneeling by his bed of death,
And Innocence is closing up his eyes,
    Now if thou wouldst, when all have given him over,
    From death to life thou mightst him yet recover.

MICHAEL DRAYTON (1563–1631)

Farewell! Thou art Too Dear for My Possessing

Farewell! thou art too dear for my possessing,
And like enough thou know'st thy estimate;
The charter of thy worth gives thee releasing;
My bonds in thee are all determinate.
For how do I hold thee but by thy granting?
And for that riches where is my deserving?
The cause of this fair gift in me is wanting,
And so my patent back again is swerving.
Thyself thou gav'st, thy own worth then not knowing,
Or me, to whom thou gav'st it, else mistaking;
So thy great gift, upon misprision growing,
Comes home again, on better judgement making.
    Thus have I had thee, as a dream doth flatter
    In sleep a king, but waking, no such matter.

WILLIAM SHAKESPEARE (1564–1616)

The Broken Heart

He is starke mad, who ever sayes
   That he hath beene in love an houre,
Yet not that love so soone decayes,
   But that it can tenne in lesse space devour;
Who will beleeve mee, if I sweare
That I have had the plague a yeare?
    Who would not laugh at mee, if I should say
    I saw a flaske of powder burne a day?

Ah, what a trifle is a heart,
   If once into Love's hands it come!
All other griefes allow a part
   To other griefes, and aske themselves but some;
They come to us, but us Love draws,
Hee swallows us, and never chawes:
    By him, as by chain'd shot, whole rankes doe dye,
    He is the tyran pike, our hearts the frye.

If 'twere not so, what did become
    Of my heart, when I first saw thee?
I brought a heart into the roome,
    But from the roome, I carried none with mee:
If it had gone to thee, I know
Mine would have taught thine heart to show
        More pitty unto mee: but Love, alas,
        At one first blow did shiver it as glasse.

Yet nothing can to nothing fall,
    Nor any place be empty quite,
Therefore I thinke my breast hath all
    Those peeces still, though they be not unite;
And now as broken glasses show
A hundred lesser faces, so
        My ragges of heart can like, wish, and adore,
        But after one such love, can love no more.

JOHN DONNE (1572–1631)

Love in a Life

Room after room,
I hunt the house through
We inhabit together.
Heart, fear nothing, for, heart, thou shalt find her –
Next time, herself! – not the trouble behind her
Left in the curtain, the couch's perfume!
As she brushed it, the cornice-wreath blossomed anew:
Yon looking-glass gleamed at the wave of her feather.

Yet the day wears,
And door succeeds door;
I try the fresh fortune –
Range the wide house from the wing to the centre.
Still the same chance! she goes out as I enter.
Spend my whole day in the quest – who cares?
But 'tis twilight, you see – with such suites to explore,
Such closets to search, such alcoves to importune!

ROBERT BROWNING (1812–89)

Love's Secret

Never seek to tell thy love,
   Love that never told can be;
For the gentle wind doth move
   Silently, invisibly.

I told my love, I told my love,
   I told her all my heart,
Trembling, cold, in ghastly fears –
   Ah! she did depart.

Soon after she was gone from me
   A traveller came by,
Silently, invisibly:
   He took her with a sigh.

WILLIAM BLAKE (1757–1827)

Why So Pale and Wan?

Why so pale and wan, fond lover?
   Prithee, why so pale?
Will, when looking well can't move her,
   Looking ill prevail?
   Prithee, why so pale?

Why so dull and mute, young sinner?
   Prithee, why so mute?
Will, when speaking well can't win her,
   Saying nothing do't?
   Prithee, why so mute?

Quit, quit for shame! This will not move;
   This cannot take her.
If of herself she will not love,
   Nothing can make her:
   The devil take her!

SIR JOHN SUCKLING (1609–42)

Dead Love

Oh, never weep for love that's dead,
Since love is seldom true
But changes his fashion from blue to red,
From brightest red to blue,
And love was born to an early death
And is so seldom true.

Then harbour no smile on your bonny face
To win the deepest sigh.
The fairest words on truest lips
Pass on and surely die,
And you will stand alone, my dear,
When wintry winds draw nigh.

Sweet, never weep for what cannot be,
For this God has not given.
If the merest dream of love were true,
Then, sweet, we should be in heaven –
And this is only earth, my dear,
Where true love is not given.

ELIZABETH SIDDAL (1829–62)

When We Two Parted

When we two parted
In silence and tears,
Half broken-hearted,
To sever for years,
Pale grew thy cheek and cold,
Colder thy kiss;
Truly that hour foretold
Sorrow to this!

The dew of the morning
Sunk chill on my brow;
It felt like the warning
Of what I feel now.
Thy vows are all broken,
And light is thy fame:
I hear thy name spoken
And share in its shame.

They name thee before me,
A knell to mine ear;
A shudder comes o'er me –
Why wert thou so dear?
They know not I knew thee
Who knew thee too well:
Long, long shall I rue thee
Too deeply to tell.

In secret we met:
In silence I grieve
That thy heart could forget,
Thy spirit deceive.
If I should meet thee
After long years,
How should I greet thee? –
With silence and tears.

GEORGE GORDON, LORD BYRON (1788–1824)

The Departure Platform

We kissed at the barrier; and passing through
She left me, and moment by moment got
Smaller and smaller, until to my view
    She was but a spot;

A wee white spot of muslin fluff
That down the diminishing platform bore
Through hustling crowds of gentle and rough
    To the carriage door.

Under the lamplight's fitful glowers,
Behind dark groups from far and near,
Whose interests were apart from ours,
    She would disappear,

Then show again, till I ceased to see
That flexible form, that nebulous white;
And she who was more than my life to me
    Had vanished quite.

We have penned new plans since that fair fond day,
And in season she will appear again –
Perhaps in the same soft white array –
      But never as then!

– 'And why, young man, must eternally fly
A joy you'll repeat, if you love her well?'
– O friend, nought happens twice thus; why,
      I cannot tell!

THOMAS HARDY (1840–1928)

At a Dinner Party

With fruit and flowers the board is deckt,
   The wine and laughter flow;
I'll not complain – could one expect
   So dull a world to know?

You look across the fruit and flowers,
  My glance your glances find.
It is our secret, only ours,
  Since all the world is blind.

AMY LEVY (1889)

Remember Thee! Remember Thee!

Remember thee! remember thee!
  Till Lethe quench life's burning stream,
Remorse and Shame shall cling to thee,
  And haunt thee like a feverish dream!

Remember thee! Aye, doubt it not.
  Thy husband too shall think of thee:
By neither shalt thou be forgot,
  Thou *false* to him, thou *fiend* to me!

GEORGE GORDON, LORD BYRON (1788–1824)

There was an Hour

In our old shipwrecked days there was an hour,
When in the firelight steadily aglow,
Joined slackly, we beheld the red chasm grow
Among the clicking coals. Our library-bower
That eve was left to us: and hushed we sat
As lovers to whom time is whispering.
From sudden-opened doors we heard them sing.
The nodding elders mixed good wine with chat.
Well knew we that life's treasure lay
With us, and of it was our talk. 'Ah, yes!
Love dies!' I said: I never thought it less.
She yearned to me that sentence to unsay.
Then when the fire domed blackening, I found
Her cheek was salt against my kiss, and swift
Up the sharp scale of sobs her breast did lift –
Now am I haunted by that taste! that sound!

GEORGE MEREDITH (1828–1909)
FROM *Modern Love*

The Chessboard

Irene, do you yet remember
Ere we were grown so sadly wise,
Those evenings in the bleak December,
Curtained warm from the snowy weather,
When you and I played chess together,
Check-mated by each other's eyes?
Ah, still I see your soft white hand
Hovering warm o'er queen and knight,
Brave pawns in valiant battle stand:
The double castles guard the wings:
The bishop, bent on distant things
Moves, sidling, through the fight,
Our fingers touch, our glances meet
And falter; falls your golden hair
Against my cheek; your bosom sweet
Is heaving. Down the field, your queen
Rides slow her soldiery all between,
And checks me unaware.

LORD LYTTON (1803–73)

Friendship after Love

After the fierce midsummer all ablaze
   Has burned itself to ashes, and expires
   In the intensity of its own fires,
There come the mellow, mild, St Martin days,
Crowned with the calm of peace, but sad with haze.
   So after love has led us, till he tires
   Of his own throes, and torments, and desires,
Comes large-eyed friendship: with a restful gaze,
He beckons us to follow, and across
   Cool verdant vales we wander free from care.
   Is it a touch of frost lies in the air?
Why are we haunted with a sense of loss?
We do not wish the pain back, or the heat;
And yet, and yet, these days are incomplete.

ELLA WHEELER WILCOX (1850–1919)

A Broken Appointment

You did not come,
And marching time drew on and wore me numb.
Yet less for loss of your dear presence there
Than that I thus found lacking in your make
That high compassion which can overbear
Reluctance for pure loving kindness' sake
Grieved I, when, as the hope-hour stroked its sum,
You did not come.

You love not me,
And love alone can lend you loyalty;
– I know and knew it. But unto the store
Of human deeds divine in all but name,
Was it not worth a little hour or more
To add yet this: Once, you, a woman, came
To soothe a time-torn man; even though it be
You love not me?

THOMAS HARDY (1840–1928)

The Night Has a Thousand Eyes

The night has a thousand eyes,
    And the day but one;
Yet the light of the bright world dies
    With the dying sun.

The mind has a thousand eyes,
    And the heart but one;
Yet the light of a whole life dies,
    When love is done.

FRANCIS WILLIAM BOURDILLON (1852–1921)

Fragment

Master in loving! till we met
I lacked the pattern thy sweet love hath set:
I hear Death's footstep – must we then forget?
Stay, stay – not yet!

GEORGE ELIOT (1819–80)

How Sleep the Brave

How Sleep the Brave

How sleep the brave, who sink to rest,
By all their country's wishes blest!
When Spring, with dewy fingers cold,
Returns to deck their hallowed mould,
She there shall dress a sweeter sod,
Than Fancy's feet have ever trod.

By fairy hands their knell is rung,
By forms unseen their dirge is sung;
There Honour comes, a pilgrim grey,
To bless the turf that wraps their clay,
And Freedom shall awhile repair,
To dwell a weeping hermit there!

WILLIAM COLLINS (1721–59)

To Lucasta, Going to the Wars

Tell me not, sweet, I am unkind,
   That from the nunnery
Of thy chaste breast and quiet mind
   To war and arms I fly.

True: a new mistress now I chase,
   The first foe in the field;
And with a stronger faith embrace
   A sword, a horse, a shield.

Yet this inconstancy is such
   As you too shall adore;
I could not love thee, dear, so much,
   Loved I not honour more.

RICHARD LOVELACE (1618–c.1657)

The War-Song of Dinas Vawr

The mountain sheep are sweeter,
But the valley sheep are fatter;
We therefore deemed it meeter
To carry off the latter;
We made an expedition,
We met a host and quelled it;
We forced a strong position,
And killed the men who held it.

On Dyfed's richest valley,
Where herds of kine were browsing,
We made a mighty sally,
To finish our carousing.
Fierce warriors rushed to meet us;
We met them and o'erthrew them:
They struggled hard to beat us;
But we conquered them and slew them.

As we drove our prize at leisure,
The king marched forth to catch us;
His rage surpassed all measure,
But his people could not match us.
He fled to his hall-pillars;
And, ere our force we led off,
Some sacked his house and cellars,
While others cut his head off.

We there, in strife bewild'ring,
Spilt blood enough to swim in:
We orphaned many children,
And widowed many women.
The eagles and the ravens
We glutted with our foemen;
The heroes and the cravens,
The spearmen and the bowmen.

We brought away from battle,
And much their land bemoaned them.

Two thousand head of cattle,
And the head of him who owned them;
Ednyfed, King of Dyfed,
His head was borne before us;
His wine and beasts supplied our feasts,
And his overthrow, our chorus.

THOMAS LOVE PEACOCK (1785–1866)

The Destruction of Sennacherib

The Assyrian came down like the wolf on the fold,
And his cohorts were gleaming in purple and gold;
And the sheen of their spears was like stars on the sea,
When the blue wave rolls nightly on deep Galilee.

Like the leaves of the forest when summer is green,
That host with their banners at sunset were seen:
Like the leaves of the forest when autumn hath blown,
That host on the morrow lay wither'd and strown.

For the Angel of Death spread his wings on the blast,
And breathed in the face of the foe as he pass'd;
And the eyes of the sleepers wax'd deadly and chill,
And their hearts but once heaved, and for ever grew still!

And there lay the steed with his nostril all wide,
But through it there roll'd not the breath of his pride;
And the foam of his gasping lay white on the turf,
And cold as the spray of the rock-beating surf.

And there lay the rider distorted and pale,
With the dew on his brow, and the rust on his mail:
And the tents were all silent, the banners alone,
The lances unlifted, the trumpet unblown.

And the widows of Ashur are loud in their wail,
And the idols are broke in the temple of Baal;
And the might of the Gentile, unsmote by the sword,
Hath melted like snow in the glance of the Lord!

GEORGE GORDON, LORD BYRON (1788–1824)

Henry V at the Siege of Harfleur

Once more unto the breach, dear friends, once more;
Or close the wall up with our English dead!
In peace there's nothing so becomes a man
As modest stillness and humility:
But when the blast of war blows in our ears,
Then imitate the action of the tiger;
Stiffen the sinews, summon up the blood,
Disguise fair nature with hard-favour'd rage;
Then lend the eye a terrible aspect;
Let it pry through the portage of the head
Like the brass cannon; let the brow o'erwhelm it
As fearfully as doth a gallèd rock
O'erhang and jutty his confounded base,
Swill'd with the wild and wasteful ocean.
Now set the teeth and stretch the nostril wide,
Hold hard the breath, and bend up every spirit
To his full height! On, on, you noblest English!
Whose blood is fet from fathers of war-proof;

Fathers that, like so many Alexanders,
Have in these parts from morn till even fought,
And sheath'd their swords for lack of argument.
Dishonour not your mothers; now attest
That those whom you call'd fathers did beget you.
Be copy now to men of grosser blood,
And teach them how to war. And you, good yeomen,
Whose limbs were made in England, show us here
The mettle of your pasture; let us swear
That you are worth your breeding; which I doubt not;
For there is none of you so mean and base
That hath not noble lustre in your eyes.
I see you stand like greyhounds in the slips,
Straining upon the start. The game's afoot:
Follow your spirit; and upon this charge
Cry, 'God for Harry! England and Saint George!'

WILLIAM SHAKESPEARE (1564–1616), *Henry V*, 3, 1

The Burial of Sir John Moore after Corruna

Not a drum was heard, not a funeral note,
As his corse to the rampart we hurried;
Not a soldier discharged his farewell shot
O'er the grave where our hero we buried.

We buried him darkly at dead of night,
The sods with our bayonets turning;
By the struggling moonbeam's misty light,
And the lantern dimly burning.

No useless coffin enclosed his breast,
Not in sheet or in shroud we wound him;
But he lay like a warrior taking his rest,
With his martial cloak around him.

Few and short were the prayers we said,
And we spoke not a word of sorrow;
But we steadfastly gazed on the face that was dead,
And we bitterly thought of the morrow.

We thought, as we hollowed his narrow bed,
And smoothed down his lonely pillow,
That the foe and the stranger would tread o'er his head,
And we far away on the billow!

Lightly they'll talk of the spirit that's gone,
And o'er his cold ashes upbraid him –
But little he'll reck, if they let him sleep on
In the grave where a Briton has laid him.

But half of our heavy task was done
When the clock struck the hour for retiring;
And we heard the distant and random gun
That the foe was sullenly firing.

Slowly and sadly we laid him down,
From the field of his fame fresh and gory;
We carved not a line, and we raised not a stone –
But we left him alone with his glory.

CHARLES WOLFE (1791–1823)

Shiloh[*]

A Requiem

Skimming lightly, wheeling still,
　　The swallows fly low
Over the field in clouded days,
　　The forest-field of Shiloh –
Over the field where April rain
Solaced the parched one stretched in pain
Through the pause of night
That followed the Sunday fight
　　Around the church of Shiloh –
The church so lone, the log-built one,
That echoed to many a parting groan
　　　And natural prayer
　　Of dying foemen mingled there –
Foemen at morn, but friends at eve –
　　Fame or country least their care:

[*] The battle at Shiloh Church in April 1862 was one of the
　　bloodiest in the American Civil War.

(What like a bullet can undeceive!)
    But now they lie low,
While over them the swallows skim,
    And all is hushed at Shiloh.

HERMAN MELVILLE (1819–81)

God Give Us Men

God give us men! A time like this demands
Strong minds, great hearts, true faith and ready
    hands!
Men whom the lust of office does not kill,
Men whom the spoils of office cannot buy,
Men who possess opinions and a will,
Men who love honour, men who cannot lie.

J. G. HOLLAND (1794–1872)

Reconciliation

Word over all, beautiful as the sky,
Beautiful that war and all its deeds of carnage must in
      time be utterly lost,
That the hands of the sisters Death and Night
      incessantly softly wash again, and ever again,
      this soiled world;
For my enemy is dead, a man divine as myself is dead,
I look where he lies, white-faced and still in the coffin
      – I draw near,
Bend down and touch lightly with my lips the white
      face in the coffin.

WALT WHITMAN (1819–92)

He was a Man

He was a man; take him for all in all,
I shall not look upon his like again.

WILLIAM SHAKESPEARE (1564–1616)

The Dying Patriot

Day breaks on England down the Kentish hills,
Singing in the silence of the meadow-footing rills,
Day of my dreams, O day!
    I saw them march from Dover, long ago,
    With a silver cross before them, singing low,
Monks of Rome from their home where the blue seas
                                  break in foam,
    Augustine with his feet of snow.

Noon strikes on England, noon on Oxford town,
Beauty she was statue cold – there's blood upon her gown:
Noon of my dreams, O noon!
    Proud and godly kings had built her, long ago,
    With her towers and tombs and statues all arow,
With her fair and floral air and the love that lingers there,
    And the streets where the great men go.

Evening on the olden, the golden sea of Wales,
When the first star shivers and the last wave pales:
O evening dreams!
   There's a house that Britons walked in, long ago,
   Where now the springs of ocean fall and flow,
And the dead robed in red and sea-lilies overhead
   Sway when the long winds blow.

Sleep not, my country: though night is here, afar
Your children of the morning are clamorous for war:
Fire in the night, O dreams!
   Though she send you as she sent you, long ago,
   South to desert, east to ocean, west to snow,
West of these out to seas colder than the Hebrides I must go,
   Where the fleet of stars is anchored and the young
                         star-captains glow.

JAMES ELROY FLECKER (1884–1915)

Safety

Dear! of all happy in the hour, most blest
   He who has found our hid security,
Assured in the dark tides of the world that rest,
   And heard our word, 'Who is so safe as we?'
We have found safety with all things undying,
   The winds, and morning, tears of men and mirth,
The deep night, and birds singing, and clouds flying,
   And sleep, and freedom, and the autumnal earth.
We have built a house that is not for time's throwing.
   We have gained a peace unshaken by pain for ever.
War knows no power. Safe shall be my going,
   Secretly armed against all death's endeavour;
Safe though all safety's lost; safe where men fall;
   And if these poor limbs die, safest of all.

RUPERT BROOKE (1887–1915)

Who Made the Law?

Who made the Law that men should die in meadows?
Who spake the word that blood should splash in lanes?
Who gave it forth that gardens should be bone-yards?
Who spread the hills with flesh, and blood, and brains?
Who made the Law?

Who made the Law that Death should stalk the village?
Who spake the word to kill among the sheaves?
Who gave it forth that death should lurk in hedgerows?
Who flung the dead among the fallen leaves?
Who made the Law?

Those who return shall find that peace endures,
Find old things old, and know the things they knew,
Walk in the garden, slumber by the fireside,
Share the peace of dawn, and dream amid the dew –
Those who return.

Those who return shall till the ancient pastures,
Clean-hearted men shall guide the plough-horse reins,
Some shall grow apples and flowers in the valleys,
Some shall go courting in summer down the lanes –
THOSE WHO RETURN.

But who made the Law? the trees shall whisper to him:
'See, see the blood – the splashes on our bark!'
Walking the meadows, he shall hear bones crackle,
And fleshless mouths shall gibber in silent lanes at dark.
Who made the Law?

Who made the Law? At noon upon the hillside
His ears shall hear a moan, his cheeks shall feel a breath,
And all along the valleys, past gardens, croft,
                              and homesteads,
HE who made the Law,
   He who made the Law,
He who made the Law shall walk along with Death.
      WHO made the Law?

LESLIE COULSON (1889–1916)

284

Into Battle

The naked earth is warm with spring,
   And with green grass and bursting trees
Leans to the sun's gaze glorying,
   And quivers in the sunny breeze;
And life is colour and warmth and light,
   And a striving evermore for these;
And he is dead who will not fight;
   And who dies fighting has increase.

The fighting man shall from the sun
   Take warmth, and life from the glowing earth;
Speed with the light-foot winds to run,
   And with the trees to newer birth;
And find, when fighting shall be done,
   Great rest, and fullness after dearth.

All the bright company of Heaven
   Hold him in their high comradeship,

The Dog-Star, and the Sisters Seven,
    Orion's Belt and sworded hip.

The woodland trees that stand together,
    They stand to him each one a friend;
They gently speak in the windy weather;
    They guide to valley and ridge's end.

The kestrel hovering by day,
    And the little owls that call by night,
Bid him be swift and keen as they,
    As keen of ear, as swift of sight.

The blackbird sings to him, 'Brother, brother,
    If this be the last song you shall sing,
Sing well, for you may not sing another;
    Brother, sing.'

In dreary, doubtful, waiting hours
    Before the brazen frenzy starts,

The horses show him nobler powers;
   O patient eyes, courageous hearts!

And when the burning moment breaks,
   And all things else are out of mind,
And only joy of battle takes
   Him by the throat, and makes him blind,

Through joy and blindness he shall know,
   Not caring much to know, that still
Nor lead nor steel shall reach him, so
   That it be not the Destined Will.

The thundering line of battle stands,
   And in the air death moans and sings;
But Day shall clasp him with strong hands,
   And Night shall fold him in soft wings.

JULIAN GRENFELL (1888–1915)

Futility

Move him into the sun –
Gently its touch awoke him once,
At home, whispering of fields unsown.
Always it woke him, even in France,
Until this morning and this snow.
If anything might rouse him now
The kind old sun will know.

Think how it wakes the seeds –
Woke, once, the clays of a cold star.
Are limbs, so dear-achieved, are sides,
Full-nerved – still warm – too hard to stir?
Was it for this the clay grew tall?
O what made fatuous sunbeams toil
To break earth's sleep at all?

WILFRED OWEN (1893–1918)

Fear No More the Heat o' the Sun

Fear no more the heat o' the sun,
Nor the furious winter's rages;
Thou thy worldly task hast done,
Home art gone and ta'en thy wages:
Golden lads and girls all must,
As chimney-sweepers, come to dust.

Fear no more the frown o' the great,
Thou art past the tyrant's stroke:
Care no more to clothe and eat;
To thee the reed is as the oak:
The sceptre, learning, physic, must
All follow this, and come to dust.

Fear no more the lightning flash,
Nor the all-dreaded thunder-stone;
Fear not slander, censure rash;
Thou hast finished joy and moan:

All lovers young, all lovers must
Consign to thee, and come to dust.

No exorciser harm thee!
Nor no witchcraft charm thee!
Ghost unlaid forbear thee!
Nothing ill come near thee!
Quiet consummation have:
And renowned be thy grave!

WILLIAM SHAKESPEARE (1564–1616), *Cymbeline, 4, 2*

The Cherry Trees

The cherry trees bend over and are shedding,
On the old road where all that passed are dead,
Their petals, strewing the grass as for a wedding
This early May morn when there is none to wed.

EDWARD THOMAS (1878–1917)

The Soldier

If I should die, think only this of me:
    That there's some corner of a foreign field
That is for ever England. There shall be
    In that rich earth a richer dust concealed;
A dust whom England bore, shaped, made aware,
    Gave, once, her flowers to love, her ways to roam,
A body of England's, breathing English air,
    Washed by the rivers, blest by suns of home.

And think, this heart, all evil shed away,
    A pulse in the eternal mind, no less
        Gives somewhere back the thoughts by
                                England given;
Her sights and sounds; dreams happy as her day;
    And laughter, learnt of friends; and gentleness,
        In hearts at peace, under an English heaven.

RUPERT BROOKE (1887–1915)

291

The Mouthless Dead

When you see millions of the mouthless dead
Across your dreams in pale battalions go.
Say not soft things as other men have said
That you'll remember. For you need not so.
Give them not praise. For, deaf, how should
                                            they know
It is not curses heaped on each gashed head?
Nor tears. Their blind eyes see not your tears flow.
Nor honour. It is easy to be dead.
Say only this, 'They are dead.' Then add thereto,
'Yet many a better one has died before.'
Then, scanning all the o'ercrowded mass, should you
Perceive one face that you loved heretofore,
It is a spook. None wears the face you knew.
Great death has made all his for evermore.

CHARLES HAMILTON SORLEY (1895–1915)

Anthem for Doomed Youth

What passing-bells for these who die as cattle?
   Only the monstrous anger of the guns.
   Only the stuttering rifles' rapid rattle
Can patter out their hasty orisons.
No mockeries for them from prayers or bells,
   Nor any voice of mourning save the choirs,
The shrill, demented choirs of wailing shells;
   And bugles calling for them from sad shires.

What candles may be held to speed them all?
   Not in the hands of boys, but in their eyes
Shall shine the holy glimmers of goodbyes.
   The pallor of girls' brows shall be their pall;
Their flowers the tenderness of silent minds,
And each slow dusk a drawing-down of blinds.

WILFRED OWEN (1893–1918)

The Dead

These hearts were woven of human joys and cares,
    Washed marvellously with sorrow, swift to mirth.
The years had given them kindness. Dawn was theirs,
    And sunset, and the colours of the earth.

These had seen movement, and heard music: known
    Slumber and waking; loved; gone proudly friended;
Felt the quick stir of wonder; sat alone;
    Touched flowers and furs and cheeks. All this is ended.

There are waters blown by changing winds to laughter
And lit by the rich skies, all day. And after,
    Frost, with a gesture, stays the waves that dance
And wandering loveliness. He leaves a white
    Unbroken glory, a gathered radiance,
A width, a shining peace, under the night.

RUPERT BROOKE (1887–1915)

FROM *Character of the Happy Warrior*

Who is the happy warrior? Who is he
That every man in arms should wish to be?
– It is the generous spirit, who, when brought
Among the tasks of real life, hath wrought
Upon the plan that pleased his boyish thought:
Whose high endeavours are an inward light
That makes the path before him always bright:
Who, with a natural instinct to discern
What knowledge can perform, is diligent to learn:
Abides by this resolve, and stops not there,
But makes his moral being his prime care;
Who, doomed to go in company with pain,
And fear, and bloodshed, miserable train!
Turns his necessity to glorious gain;
In face of these doth exercise a power
Which is our human nature's highest dower;
Controls them and subdues, transmutes, bereaves
Of their bad influence, and their good receives:

By objects, which might force the soul to abate
Her feeling, rendered more compassionate;
Is placable – because occasions rise
So often that demand such sacrifice;
More skilful in self-knowledge, even more pure,
As tempted more; more able to endure,
As more exposed to suffering and distress;
Thence, also, more alive to tenderness.
– 'Tis he whose law is reason; who depends
Upon that law as on the best of friends;
Whence, in a state where men are tempted still
To evil for a guard against worse ill,
And what in quality or act is best
Doth seldom on a right foundation rest,
He labours good on good to fix, and owes
To virtue every triumph that he knows . . .
This is the happy warrior; this is he
That every man in arms should wish to be.

WILLIAM WORDSWORTH (1770–1850)

The Soldier

'Tis strange to look on a man that is dead
As he lies in the shell-swept hell,
And to think that the poor black battered corpse
Once lived like you and was well.

'Tis stranger far when you come to think
That you may be soon like him . . .
And it's Fear that tugs at your trembling soul,
A Fear that is weird and grim!

A. J. MANN (1896-1917)

War

Where war has left its wake of whitened bone,
Soft stems of summer grass shall wave again,
And all the blood that war has ever strewn
        Is but a passing stain.

LESLIE COULSON (1889–1916)

In Flanders Fields

In Flanders fields the poppies blow
Between the crosses, row on row,
   That mark our place; and in the sky
   The larks, still bravely singing, fly
Scarce heard amid the guns below.

We are the Dead. Short days ago
We lived, felt dawn, saw sunset glow,
   Loved and were loved, and now we lie
      In Flanders fields.

Take up our quarrel with the foe:
To you from failing hands we throw
   The torch; be yours to hold it high.
   If ye break faith with us who die
We shall not sleep, though poppies grow
      In Flanders fields.

JOHN McCRAE (1872–1918)

Something Far More Deeply Interfused

A Sense Sublime

For I have learned
To look on nature, not as in the hour
Of thoughtless youth, but hearing oftentimes
The still, sad music of humanity,
Nor harsh nor grating, though of ample power
To chasten and subdue. And I have felt
A presence that disturbs me with the joy
Of elevated thoughts; a sense sublime
Of something far more deeply interfused,
Whose dwelling is the light of setting suns,

And the round ocean, and the living air,
And the blue sky, and in the mind of man,
A motion and a spirit, that impels
All thinking things, all objects of all thought,
And rolls through all things. Therefore am I still
A lover of the meadows and the woods
And mountains; and of all that we behold
From this green earth; of all the mighty world
Of eye and ear, both what they half-create,
And what perceive; well pleased to recognise
In nature and the language of the sense,
The anchor of my purest thoughts, the nurse,
The guide, the guardian of my heart, and soul
Of all my moral being.

WILLIAM WORDSWORTH (1770–1850)

FROM *Lines Written a Few Miles above Tintern Abbey*

Uphill

Does the road wind uphill all the way?
  Yes, to the very end.
Will the day's journey take the whole long day?
  From morn to night, my friend.

But is there for the night a resting-place?
  A roof for when the slow, dark hours begin.
May not the darkness hide it from my face?
  You cannot miss that inn.

Shall I meet other wayfarers at night?
  Those who have gone before.
Then must I knock, or call when just in sight?
  They will not keep you standing at that door.

Shall I find comfort, travel-sore and weak?
  Of labour you shall find the sum.
Will there be beds for me and all who seek?
  Yea, beds for all who come.

CHRISTINA ROSSETTI (1830–94)

On being Questioned about the
Nature of the Sacrament

Christ was the Word and spake it;
He took the bread and brake it;
And what the Word did make it,
That I believe and take it.

attributed to **QUEEN ELIZABETH I (1533–1603)**

In No Strange Land

O world invisible, we view thee,
O world intangible, we touch thee,
O world unknowable, we know thee,
Inapprehensible, we clutch thee!

Does the fish soar to find the ocean,
The eagle plunge to find the air –

That we ask of the stars in motion
If they have rumour of thee there?

Not where the wheeling systems darken,
And our benumb'd conceiving soars! –
The drift of pinions, would we hearken,
Beats at our own clay-shutter'd doors.

The angels keep their ancient places –
Turn but a stone, and start a wing!
'Tis ye, 'tis your estrangèd faces,
That miss the many-splendour'd thing.

But (when so sad thou canst not sadder)
Cry – and upon thy so sore loss
Shall shine the traffic of Jacob's ladder,
Pitched betwixt Heaven and Charing Cross.

Yea, in the night, my soul, my daughter,
Cry – clinging Heaven by the hems;
And lo, Christ walking on the water,
Not of Gennesareth, but Thames!

FRANCIS THOMPSON (1859–1907)

Pied Beauty

Glory be to God for dappled things –
   For skies of couple-colour as a brinded cow;
     For rose-moles all in stipple upon trout that swim;
Fresh-firecoal chestnut-falls; finches' wings;
   Landscape plotted and pieced – fold, fallow,
                    and plough;
    And áll trádes, their gear and tackle and trim.

All things counter, original, spare, strange;
   Whatever is fickle, freckled (who knows how?)
    With swift, slow; sweet, sour; adazzle, dim;
He fathers-forth whose beauty is past change:
      Praise him.

GERARD MANLEY HOPKINS (1844–89)

Virtue

Sweet day, so cool, so calm, so bright,
The bridal of the earth and sky;
The dew shall weep thy fall tonight,
            For thou must die.

Sweet rose, whose hue angry and brave
Bids the rash gazer wipe his eye,
Thy root is ever in its grave,
            And thou must die.

Sweet spring, full of sweet days and roses,
A box where sweets compacted lie;
My music shows ye have your closes,
            And all must die.

Only a sweet and virtuous soul,
Like season'd timber, never gives;
But though the whole world turn to coal,
            Then chiefly lives.

GEORGE HERBERT (1596–1633)

God Moves in a Mysterious Way

God moves in a mysterious way,
    His wonders to perform;
He plants his footsteps in the sea,
    And rides upon the storm.

Deep in unfathomable mines
    Of never-failing skill
He treasures up his bright designs,
    And works his sovereign will.

Ye fearful saints, fresh courage take,
    The clouds ye so much dread
Are big with mercy, and shall break
    In blessings on your head.

Judge not the Lord by feeble sense,
    But trust him for his grace;
Behind a frowning providence,
    He hides a smiling face.

His purposes will ripen fast,
　　Unfolding ev'ry hour;
The bud may have a bitter taste,
　　But sweet will be the flow'r.

Blind unbelief is sure to err,
　　And scan his work in vain;
God is his own interpreter,
　　And he will make it plain.

WILLIAM COWPER (1731–1800)

From David's Lips this Word did Roll

From David's lips this word did roll,
'Tis true and living yet:
No man can save his brother's soul,
Nor pay his brother's debt.

MATTHEW ARNOLD (1822–88)

A Little Learning is a Dangerous Thing

A little learning is a dangerous thing;
Drink deep, or taste not the Pierian spring:
There shallow draughts intoxicate the brain,
And drinking largely sobers us again.
Fired at first sight with what the Muse imparts,
In fearless youth we tempt the heights of arts,
While from the bounded level of our mind
Short views we take, nor see the lengths behind;
But more advanced, behold with strange surprise
New distant scenes of endless science rise!
So pleased at first the towering Alps we try,
Mount o'er the vales, and seem to tread the sky,
The eternal snows appear already pass'd,
And the first clouds and mountains seem the last:
But, those attain'd, we tremble to survey
The growing labours of the lengthen'd way,
The increasing prospect tires our wandering eyes,
Hills peep o'er hills, and Alps on Alps arise!

ALEXANDER POPE (1688–1744)

FROM *An Essay on Criticism*

The Foil

  If we could see below
The sphere of virtue and each shining grace
  As plainly as that above doth show,
This were the better sky, the brighter place.

  God hath made stars the foil
To set off virtues, griefs to set off sinning;
  Yet in this wretched world we toil,
As if grief were not foul, nor virtue winning.

         GEORGE HERBERT (1596–1633)

O Fret Not after Knowledge!

O fret not after knowledge – I have none,
And yet my song comes native with the warmth.
O fret not after knowledge – I have none,
And yet the evening listens.

         JOHN KEATS (1795–1821)

Say Not the Struggle Nought Availeth

Say not the struggle nought availeth,
    The labour and the wounds are vain,
The enemy faints not, nor faileth,
    And as things have been, things remain.

If hopes were dupes, fears may be liars;
    It may be, in yon smoke concealed,
Your comrades chase e'en now the fliers,
    And, but for you, possess the field.

For while the tired waves, vainly breaking,
    Seem here no painful inch to gain,
Far back through creeks and inlets making
    Came, silent, flooding in, the main,

And not by eastern windows only,
    When daylight comes, comes in the light,
In front the sun climbs slow, how slowly,
    But westward, look, the land is bright.

ARTHUR HUGH CLOUGH (1819–61)

When I Have Fears that I May Cease To Be

When I have fears that I may cease to be
   Before my pen has gleaned my teeming brain,
Before high-pilèd books, in charactery,
   Hold like full garners the full-ripened grain;
When I behold, upon the night's starred face,
   Huge cloudy symbols of a high romance,
And feel that I may never live to trace
   Their shadows, with the magic hand of chance;
And when I feel, fair creature of an hour!
   That I shall never look upon thee more,
Never have relish in the faery power
   Of unreflecting love – then on the shore
Of the wide world I stand alone, and think,
Till Love and Fame to nothingness do sink.

JOHN KEATS (1795–1821)

Somewhere or Other

Somewhere or other there must surely be
    The face not seen, the voice not heard,
The heart that not yet – never yet – ah me!
    Made answer to my word.

Somewhere or other, maybe near or far;
    Past land and sea, clean out of sight;
Beyond the wandering moon, beyond the star
    That tracks her night by night.

Somewhere or other, maybe far or near;
    With just a wall, a hedge, between;
With just the last leaves of the dying year
    Fallen on a turf grown green.

CHRISTINA ROSSETTI (1830–94)

On His Blindness

When I consider how my light is spent
   Ere half my days, in this dark world and wide,
   And that one talent which is death to hide,
Lodged with me useless, though my soul more bent
To serve therewith my Maker, and present
   My true account, lest he, returning, chide;
   'Doth God exact day-labour, light denied?'
I fondly ask: but Patience, to prevent
   That murmur, soon replies, 'God doth not need
Either man's work, or his own gifts; who best
    Bear his mild yoke, they serve him best; his state
   Is kingly: thousands at his bidding speed,
And post o'er land and ocean without rest;
    They also serve who only stand and wait.'

JOHN MILTON (1608–74)

On First Looking into Chapman's Homer

Much have I travelled in the realms of gold,
   And many goodly states and kingdoms seen;
   Round many western islands have I been
Which bards in fealty to Apollo hold.
Oft of one wide expanse had I been told
   That deep-brow'd Homer ruled as his demesne:
   Yet did I never breathe its pure serene
Till I heard Chapman speak out loud and bold:
Then felt I like some watcher of the skies
   When a new planet swims into his ken;
Or like stout Cortez, when with eagle eyes
   He stared at the Pacific – and all his men
Looked at each other with a wild surmise –
   Silent, upon a peak in Darien.

JOHN KEATS (1795–1821)

It Fortifies My Soul to Know

It fortifies my soul to know
That, though I perish, truth is so;
That, howsoe'er I stay or range,
Whate'er I do, Thou dost not change.
I steadier step when I recall
That, if I slip, Thou dost not fall.

ARTHUR HUGH CLOUGH (1891–61)

Patience

Patience! why 'tis the soul of peace:
Of all the virtues, 'tis nearest kin to heaven:
It makes men look like gods. The best of men
That e'er wore earth about Him was a sufferer,
A soft, meek, patient, humble, tranquil spirit:
The first true gentleman that ever breathed.

THOMAS DEKKER (c.1570–c.1641)

Waiting Both

A star looks down on me,
And says, 'Here I and you
Stand, each in our degree:
What do you mean to do –
    Mean to do?'

I say: 'For all I know,
Wait, and let time go by,
Till my change come.' 'Just so,'
The star says. 'So mean I –
    So mean I.'

THOMAS HARDY (1840–1928)

Hamlet's Soliloquy

To be, or not to be: that is the question:
Whether 'tis nobler in the mind to suffer
The slings and arrows of outrageous fortune,
Or to take arms against a sea of troubles,
And by opposing end them? To die: to sleep;
No more; and, by a sleep to say we end
The heartache and the thousand natural shocks
That flesh is heir to, 'tis a consummation
Devoutly to be wish'd. To die, to sleep;
To sleep: perchance to dream: ay, there's the rub;
For in that sleep of death what dreams may come,
When we have shuffled off this mortal coil,
Must give us pause. There's the respect
That makes calamity of so long life;
For who would bear the whips and scorns of time,
The oppressor's wrong, the proud man's contumely,
The pangs of dispriz'd love, the law's delay,
The insolence of office, and the spurns

That patient merit of the unworthy takes,
When he himself might his quietus make
With a bare bodkin? who would fardels bear,
To grunt and sweat under a weary life,
But that the dread of something after death,
The undiscover'd country from whose bourn
No traveller returns, puzzles the will,
And makes us rather bear those ills we have
Than fly to others that we know not of?
Thus conscience doth make cowards of us all;
And thus the native hue of resolution
Is sicklied o'er with the pale cast of thought,
And enterprises of great pith and moment
With this regard their currents turn awry,
And lose the name of action.

WILLIAM SHAKESPEARE (1564–1616), *Hamlet*, 3, 1

He That is Down Needs Fear No Fall

He that is down needs fear no fall,
   He that is low, no pride;
He that is humble ever shall
   Have God to be his guide.

I am content with what I have,
   Little be it or much:
And, Lord, contentment still I crave;
   Because Thou savest such.

Fullness to such a burden is
   That go on pilgrimage:
Here little, and hereafter bliss,
   Is best from age to age.

JOHN BUNYAN (1628–88)

The Pilgrim

Who would true valour see,
    Let him come hither!
One here will constant be,
    Come wind, come weather;
There's no discouragement
Shall make him once relent
His first avowed intent
    To be a pilgrim.

Whoso beset him round
    With dismal stories
Do but themselves confound,
    His strength the more is.
No lion can him fright;
He'll with a giant fight;
But he will have a right
    To be a pilgrim.

Nor enemy, nor friend,
    Can daunt his spirit;
He knows he at the end
    Shall life inherit:
Then, fancies, fly away;
He'll fear not what men say;
He'll labour, night and day,
    To be a pilgrim.

JOHN BUNYAN (1628–88)

Alas! How Easily Things Go Wrong!

Alas! how easily things go wrong!
A sigh too much or a kiss too long;
And there follows a mist and a weeping rain
And life is never the same again.

GEORGE MACDONALD (1824–1905)

Introspective

I wish it were over, the terrible pain,
Pang after pang, again and again;
First the shattering ruining blow,
Then the probing steady and slow.

Did I wince? I did not faint:
My soul broke but was not bent:
Up I stand like a blasted tree
By the shore of the shivering sea.

On my boughs neither leaf nor fruit,
No sap in my utmost root,
Brooding in an anguish dumb
On the short past and the long to-come.

Dumb I was when the ruin fell,
Dumb I remain and will never tell;
Oh my soul, I talk with thee,
But not another the sight must see.

I did not start when the torture stung,
I did not faint when the torture wrung;
Let it come tenfold if come it must,
But I will not groan when I bite the dust.

CHRISTINA ROSSETTI (1830–94)

The Adventurer

Give me a spirit that on this life's rough sea
Loves to have his sails filled with a lusty wind,
Even till his sail-yards tremble, his masts crack,
And his rapt ship run on her side so low
That she drinks water, and her keel ploughs air.

GEORGE CHAPMAN (c.1559–1634)

Hymn

O God, our help in ages past,
   Our hope for years to come,
Our shelter from the stormy blast,
   And our eternal home.

Beneath the shadow of thy throne
   Thy saints have dwelt secure;
Sufficient is thine arm alone,
   And our defence is sure.

Before the hills in order stood,
   Or earth received her frame.
From everlasting thou art God,
   To endless years the same.

Thy Word commands our flesh to dust,
   Return, ye sons of men:
All nations rose from earth at first,
   And turn to earth again.

A thousand ages in thy sight
   Are like an evening gone;

Short as the watch that ends the night
  Before the rising sun.

The busy tribes of flesh and blood
  With all their lives and cares
Are carried downwards by thy flood,
  And lost in following years.

Time like an ever-rolling stream
  Bears all its sons away;
They fly forgotten as a dream
  Dies at the opening day.

Like flowery fields the nations stand
  Pleased with the morning-light;
The flowers beneath the mower's hand
  Lie withering ere 'tis night.

O God, our help in ages past,
  Our hope for years to come,
Be thou our guard while troubles last,
  And our eternal home.

ISSAC WATTS (1674–1748)

Drowning is Not So Pitiful

Drowning is not so pitiful
   As the attempt to rise.
Three times, 'tis said, a sinking man
   Comes up to face the skies,
And then declines forever
   To that abhorred abode
Where hope and he part company –
   For he is grasped of God.
The Maker's cordial visage,
   However good to see,
Is shunned, we must admit it,
   Like an adversity.

EMILY DICKINSON (1830–86)

Dover Beach

The sea is calm tonight,
The tide is full, the moon lies fair
Upon the Straits! on the French coast, the light
Gleams and is gone! the cliffs of England stand
Glimmering and vast, out in the tranquil bay.
Come to the window, sweet is the night air!
Only from the long line of spray,
Where the ebb meets the moon-blanched sand,
Listen! you hear the grating roar
Of pebbles which the waves suck back and fling,
At their return, up the high strand,
Begin and cease, and then again begin
With tremulous cadence slow, and bring
The eternal note of sadness in.

Sophocles long ago
Heard it on the Aegean, and it brought
Into his mind the turbid ebb and flow
Of human misery: we

Find also in the sound a thought,
Hearing it by this distant northern sea.

The sea of faith
Was once, too, at the full, and round earth's shore
Lay like the folds of a bright girdle furled:
But now I only hear
Its melancholy long, withdrawing roar,
Retreating to the breath
Of the night wind down the vast edges drear
And naked shingles of the world.

Ah, love! let us be true
To one another! for the world, which seems
To lie before us like a land of dreams,
So various, so beautiful, so new,
Hath really neither joy, nor love, nor light,
Nor certitude, nor peace, nor help for pain:
And we are here, as on a darkling plain
Swept with confused alarms of struggle and flight,
Where ignorant armies clash by night.

MATTHEW ARNOLD (1822–88)

The Seas are Quiet

The seas are quiet when the winds give o'er;
So calm are we when passions are no more.
For then we know how vain it was to boast
Of fleeting things, so certain to be lost.
Clouds of affection from our younger eyes
Conceal that emptiness which age descries.

The soul's dark cottage, batter'd and decay'd,
Lets in new light through chinks that time hath made:
Stronger by weakness, wiser men become
As they draw near to their eternal home.
Leaving the old, both worlds at once they view
That stand upon the threshold of the new.

EDMUND WALLER (1606–87)

Parting at Morning

Round the cape of a sudden came the sea,
And the sun looked over the mountain's rim –
And straight was a path of gold for him,
And the need of a world of men for me.

ROBERT BROWNING (1812–89)

A Farewell

'And if I did, what then?
  Are you aggrieved therefore?
The sea hath fish for every man,
  And what would you have more?'

Thus did my mistress once
  Amaze my mind with doubt;
And popped a question for the nonce,
  To beat my brains about.

330

Whereto I thus replied:
   'Each fisherman can wish,
That all the seas at every tide
   Were his alone to fish.

'And so did I in vain.
   But since it may not be,
Let such fish there as find the gain,
   And leave the loss for me.

'And with such luck and loss
   I will content myself,
Till tides of turning time may toss
   Such fishers on the shelf.

'And when they stick on sands,
   That every man may see,
Then will I laugh and clap my hands,
   As they do now at me.'

GEORGE GASCOIGNE (1542–77)

There Came a Wind Like a Bugle

There came a wind like a bugle;
It quivered through the grass,
And a green chill upon the heat
So ominous did pass
We barred the windows and the doors
As from an emerald ghost;
The doom's electric moccasin
That very instant passed.
On a strange mob of panting trees,
And fences fled away,

And rivers where the houses ran
The living looked that day.
The bell within the steeple wild
The flying tidings whirled.
How much can come
And much can go,
And yet abide the world!

EMILY DICKINSON (1830–86)

Windmill

At eve thou loomest like a one-eyed giant
To some poor crazy knight, who pricks along
And sees thee wave in haze thy arms defiant,
And growl the burden of thy grinding song.

Against thy russet sail-sheet slowly turning,
The raven beats belated in the blast:
Behind thee ghastly, blood-red eve is burning,
Above, rose-feathered drifts are racking fast.

The curlews pipe around their plaintive dirges,
Thou art a Pharos to the sea-mews hoar,
Set sheer above the tumult of the surges,
As sea-mark on some spacious ocean floor.

My heart is sick with gazing on thy feature,
Old blackened sugar-loaf with fourfold wings,
Thou seemest as some monstrous insect creature,
Some mighty chafer armed with iron stings.

Emblem of man who, after all his moaning,
And strain of dire immeasurable strife,
Has yet this consolation, all atoning –
Life, as a windmill grinds the bread of Life.

LORD DE TABLEY (1835–95)

Heaven–Haven

A nun takes the veil

I have desired to go
   Where springs not fail,
To fields where flies no sharp and sided hail
   And a few lilies blow.

And I have asked to be
   Where no storms come,
Where the green swell is in the havens dumb,
   And out of the swing of the sea.

GERARD MANLEY HOPKINS (1845–89)

Lead, Kindly Light!

Lead, kindly Light, amid the encircling gloom,
    Lead thou me on;
The night is dark, and I am far from home,
    Lead thou me on.
Keep thou my feet; I do not ask to see
The distant scene; one step enough for me.

I was not ever thus, nor prayed that thou
    Shouldst lead me on;
I loved to choose and see my path; but now
    Lead thou me on.
I loved the garish day, and, spite of fears,
Pride ruled my will: remember not past years.

So long thy power hath blest me, sure it still
    Will lead me on,
O'er moor and fen, o'er crag and torrent, till
    The night is gone;
And with the morn those angel faces smile,
Which I have loved long since, and lost awhile.

JOHN HENRY NEWMAN (1801–90)

He Prayeth Best

Farewell, farewell! but this I tell
To thee, thou wedding-guest!
He prayeth well who loveth well
Both man and bird and beast.

He prayeth best who loveth best
All things both great and small;
For the dear God, who loveth us,
He made and loveth all.

SAMUEL TAYLOR COLERIDGE (1772–1834)
FROM *The Rime of the Ancient Mariner*

A Fine Invention

Faith is a fine invention
For gentlemen who see;
But microscopes are prudent
In an emergency!

EMILY DICKINSON (1830–86)

The Guiding Lamp

Silent is the house: all are laid asleep:
One alone looks out o'er the snow-wreaths deep,
Watching every cloud, dreading every breeze
That whirls the wildering drift and bends the
                                    groaning trees.

Cheerful is the hearth, soft the matted floor:
Not one shivering gust creeps through pane or door:
The little lamp burns straight, its rays shoot
                                    strong and far:
I trim it well to be the wanderer's guiding star.

Frown, my haughty sire: chide, my angry dame;
Set your slaves to spy: threaten me with shame!
But neither sire nor dame nor prying serf shall know
What angel nightly tracks that waste of frozen snow.

What I love shall come like visitant of air,
Safe in secret power from lurking human snare:

What loves me no word of mine shall e'er betray,
Though for faith unstained my life must forfeit pay.

Burn, then, little lamp: glimmer straight and clear –
Hush! a rustling wing stirs, methinks, the air:
He for whom I wait thus ever comes to me:
Strange Power! I trust thy might: trust thou
                                        my constancy.

EMILY BRONTË (1818–48)

Creation's Voice

The spacious firmament on high,
With all the blue ethereal sky,
And spangled heav'ns, a shining frame,
Their great Original proclaim.
Th'unwearied sun, from day to day,
Doth his Creator's power display,
And publishes to every land
The work of an Almighty Hand.

Soon as the evening shades prevail,
The moon takes up the wondrous tale,
And nightly to the listening earth
Repeats the story of her birth;
While all the stars that round her burn,
And all the planets in their turn,
Confirm the tidings, as they roll,
And spread the truth from pole to pole.

What though in solemn silence all
Move round the dark terrestrial ball?
What though no real voice or sound
Amidst their radiant orbs be found?

In reason's ear they all rejoice,
And utter forth a glorious voice,
For ever singing, as they shine,
'The Hand that made us is Divine.'

JOSEPH ADDISON (1672–1719)

Failure

Because God put His adamantine fate
    Between my sullen heart and its desire,
I swore that I would burst the iron gate,
    Rise up, and curse Him on His throne of fire.
Earth shuddered at my crown of blasphemy,
    But love was as a flame about my feet;
Proud up the golden stair I strode; and beat
    Thrice on the gate, and entered with a cry –

All the great courts were quiet in the sun,
    And full of vacant echoes: moss had grown
Over the glassy pavement, and begun
    To creep within the dusty council-halls.
An idle wind blew round an empty throne
    And stirred the heavy curtains on the walls.

RUPERT BROOKE (1887–1915)

The Oxen

Christmas Eve, and twelve of the clock.
   'Now they are all on their knees,'
An elder said as we sat in a flock
   By the embers in hearthside ease.

We pictured the meek mild creatures where
   They dwelt in their strawy pen,
Nor did it occur to one of us there
   To doubt they were kneeling then.

So fair a fancy few would weave
   In these years! Yet, I feel,
If someone said on Christmas Eve,
   'Come; see the oxen kneel

In the lonely barton by yonder coomb
   Our childhood used to know,'
I should go with him in the gloom,
   Hoping it might be so.

THOMAS HARDY (1840–1928)

341

On Being Brought from Africa to America

'Twas mercy brought me from my pagan land,
Taught my benighted soul to understand
That there's a God, that there's a Saviour too:
Once I redemption neither sought nor knew.
Some view our sable race with scornful eye:
'Their colour is a diabolic dye.'
Remember, Christians, negroes black as Cain
May be refined and join the angelic train.

PHILLIS WHEATLEY (*c.*1753–84)

Not Knowing

Not knowing when the dawn will come
I open every door.
Or has it feathers like a bird,
Or billows like a shore?

EMILY DICKINSON (1830–86)

Spellbound

The night is darkening round me,
The wild winds coldly blow;
But a tyrant spell has bound me
And I cannot, cannot go.

The giant trees are bending
Their bare boughs weighed with snow.
And the storm is fast descending,
And yet I cannot go.

Clouds beyond clouds above me,
Wastes beyond wastes below;
But nothing drear can move me;
I will not, cannot go.

EMILY BRONTË (1818–48)

At the Last

When on my day of life the night is falling,
    And, in the winds from unsunned spaces blown,
I hear far voices out of darkness calling
    My feet to paths unknown;

Thou who hast made my home of life so pleasant,
    Leave not its tenant when its walls decay;
O Love Divine, O Helper ever present,
    Be Thou my strength and stay.

Be near me when all else is from me drifting –
    Earth, sky, home's pictures, days of shade and shine,
And kindly faces to my own uplifting
    The love which answers mine.

I have but Thee, my Father! let Thy Spirit
    Be with me then to comfort and uphold;
No gate of pearl, no branch of palm I merit,
    Nor streets of shining gold.

Suffice it if – my good and ill unreckoned,
    And both forgiven through Thy abounding grace –

I find myself by hands familiar beckoned
    Unto my fitting place:

Some humble door among Thy many mansions,
    Some sheltering shade where sin and striving cease,
And flows for ever through heaven's green expansions
    The river of Thy peace.

There, from the music round about me stealing.
    I fain would learn the new and holy song,
And find at last, beneath Thy trees of healing,
    The life for which I long.

JOHN GREENLEAF WHITTIER (1807–92)

Parting

My life closed twice before its close;
    It yet remains to see
If Immortality unveil
    A third event to me.

So huge, so hopeless to conceive,
    As these that twice befell.
Parting is all we know of heaven,
And all we need of hell.

EMILY DICKINSON (1830–86)

Contradictions

Now, even, I cannot think it true,
My friend, that there is no more you.
Almost as soon were no more I,
Which were of course absurdity!

Your place is bare, you are not seen,
Your grave, I'm told, is growing green;
And both for you and me, you know,
There's no Above and no Below.
That you are dead must be inferred,
And yet my thought rejects the word.

AMY LEVY (1861–89)

Some Future Day

Some future day, when what is now is not,
When all our faults and follies are forgot,
And thought of difference passed like dreams away,
We'll meet again, upon some future day.

When all that hindered, all that vexed our love,
As tall rank weeds will climb the blade above,
When all but it has yielded to decay,
We'll meet again upon some future day.

When we have passed, each on his course alone
The wider world and learned what's now unknown,
Have made life clear and worked out each a way,
We'll meet again – we shall have much to say.

With happier mood, and feelings born anew,
Our boyhood's bygone fancies we'll review,
Talk o'er old talks, play as we used to play
And meet again, on many a future day.

Some day, which oft our hearts shall yearn to see,
In some far year, though distant, yet to be,
Shall we indeed – ye winds and waters, say! –
Meet yet again, upon some future day?

ARTHUR HUGH CLOUGH (1819–61)

Surgeons Must be Very Careful

Surgeons must be very careful
When they take the knife!
Underneath their fine incisions
Stirs the Culprit – *Life*.

EMILY DICKINSON (1830–86)

We Die in Earnest,
That's No Jest

What is Our Life?

What is our life? A play of passion,
Our mirth the music of division.
Our mother's wombs the tiring-houses be,
Where we are dressed for this short comedy.
Heaven the judicious sharp spectator is,
Who sits and marks still who doth act amiss.
Our graves that hide us from the searching sun
Are like drawn curtains when the play is done.
Thus march we, playing, to our latest rest,
Only we die in earnest, that's no jest.

SIR WALTER RALEIGH (1552–1618)

Surprised by Joy – Impatient as the Wind

Surprised by joy – impatient as the wind,
I wished to share the transport – Oh! with whom
But thee, long buried in the silent tomb,
That spot which no vicissitude can find?
Love, faithful love, recalled thee to my mind –
But how could I forget thee! Through what power,
Even for the least division of an hour,
Have I been so beguiled as to be blind
To my most grievous loss? – That thought's return
Was the worst pang that sorrow ever bore,
Save one, one only, when I stood forlorn,
Knowing my heart's best treasure was no more;
That neither present time, nor years unborn,
Could to my sight that heavenly face restore.

WILLIAM WORDSWORTH (1770–1850)

Epitaph to Sir William Dyer

My dearest dust, could not thy hasty day
Afford thy drowsy patience leave to stay
One hour longer: so that we might either
Sat up, or gone to bed together?
But since thy finished labour hath possessed
Thy weary limbs with early rest,
Enjoy it sweetly: and thy widow bride
Shall soon repose her by thy slumbering side.
Whose business, now, is only to prepare
My nightly dress, and call to prayer:
Mine eyes wax heavy and ye day grows old,
The dew falls thick, my beloved grows cold.
Draw, draw ye closèd curtains: and make room:
My dear, my dearest dust; I come, I come.

CATHERINE, LADY DYER (1641)

To —

Music, when soft voices die,
Vibrates in the memory –
Odours, when sweet violets sicken,
Live within the sense they quicken.

Rose leaves, when the rose is dead,
Are heaped for the belovèd's bed;
And so thy thoughts, when thou art gone,
Love itself shall slumber on.

PERCY BYSSHE SHELLEY (1792–1822)

Macbeth on Lady Macbeth's Death

Tomorrow, and tomorrow, and tomorrow,
Creeps in this petty pace from day to day,
To the last syllable of recorded time;
And all our yesterdays have lighted fools
The way to dusty death. Out, out, brief candle!

Life's but a walking shadow, a poor player
That struts and frets his hour upon the stage,
And then is heard no more; it is a tale
Told by an idiot, full of sound and fury,
Signifying nothing.

WILLIAM SHAKESPEARE (1564–1616), *Macbeth*, 5, 5

A Quiet Soul

Thy soul within such silent pomp did keep
    As if humanity were lulled asleep;
So gentle was thy pilgrimage beneath,
    Time's unheard feet scarce make less noise,
    Or the soft journey which a planet goes.
Life seemed all calm as its last breath,
    A still tranquillity so hushed thy breast,
    As if some Halcyon were its guest,
    And there had built her nest;
It hardly now enjoys a greater rest.

JOHN OLDHAM (1653–83)

Silence

There is a silence where hath been no sound,
   There is a silence where no sound may be,
   In the cold grave, under the deep, deep sea
Or in wide desert where no life is found,
Which hath been mute, and still must sleep profound;
   No voice is hushed – no life treads silently,
   But clouds and cloudy shadows wander free,
That never spoke, over the idle ground:
But in green ruins, in the desolate walls
   Of antique palaces where Man hath been,
Though the dun fox, or wild hyena, calls,
   And owls, that flit continually between,
Shriek to the echo, and the low winds moan,
There the true silence is, self-conscious and alone.

THOMAS HOOD (1799–1845)

When I am Dead, My Dearest

When I am dead, my dearest,
Sing no sad songs for me;
Plant thou no roses at my head,
Nor shady cypress tree:
Be the green grass above me
With showers and dewdrops wet:
And if thou wilt, remember,
And if thou wilt, forget.

I shall not see the shadows,
I shall not feel the rain;
I shall not hear the nightingale
Sing on as if in pain:
And dreaming through the twilight
That doth not rise nor set,
Haply I may remember,
And haply may forget.

CHRISTINA ROSSETTI (1830–94)

No Coward Soul is Mine

No coward soul is mine,
No trembler in the world's storm-troubled sphere:
I see Heaven's glories shine,
And Faith shines equal, arming me from fear.

O God within my breast,
Almighty, ever-present Deity!
Life – that in me has rest,
As I – undying Life – have power in thee!

Vain are the thousand creeds
That move men's hearts, unutterably vain;
Worthless as withered weeds
Or idlest froth amid the boundless main

To waken doubt in one
Holding so fast by thy infinity;
So surely anchored on
The steadfast rock of Immortality.

With wide-embracing love
Thy spirit animates eternal years,
Pervades and broods above,
Changes, sustains, dissolves, creates and rears.

Though earth and moon were gone,
And suns and universe ceased to be,
And thou were left alone,
Every existence would exist in thee.

There is not room for Death,
Nor atom that his might could render void:
Since thou art Being and Breath,
And what thou art may never be destroyed.

EMILY BRONTË (1818–48)

FROM *The Ballad of Reading Gaol*

He did not wear his scarlet coat,
  For blood and wine are red,
And blood and wine were on his hands
  When they found him with the dead,
The poor dead woman whom he loved,
  And murdered in her bed.

He walked amongst the trial men
  In a suit of shabby grey;
A cricket cap was on his head,
  And his step seemed light and gay;
But I never saw a man who looked
  So wistfully at the day.

I never saw a man who looked
  With such a wistful eye
Upon that little tent of blue
  Which prisoners call the sky,
And at every drifting cloud that went
  With sails of silver by.

I walked, with other souls in pain,
   Within another ring,
And was wondering if the man had done
   A great or little thing,
When a voice behind me whispered low,
   'That fellow's got to swing.'

Dear Christ! the very prison walls
   Suddenly seemed to reel,
And the sky above my head became
   Like a casque of scorching steel;
And, though I was a soul in pain,
   My pain I could not feel.

I only knew what hunted thought
   Quickened his step, and why
He looked upon the garish day
   With such a wistful eye;
The man had killed the thing he loved,
   And so he had to die.

*   *   *

Yet each man kills the thing he loves,
    By each let this be heard,
Some do it with a bitter look,
    Some with a flattering word,
The coward does it with a kiss,
    The brave man with a sword!

Some kill their love when they are young
    And some when they are old;
Some strangle with the hands of lust,
    Some with the hands of gold:
The kindest use a knife, because
    The dead so soon grow cold.

Some love too little, some too long,
    Some sell, and others buy;
Some do the deed with many tears,
    And some without a sigh:
For each man kills the thing he loves,
    Yet each man does not die.

He does not die a death of shame
   On a day of dark disgrace,
Nor have a noose about his neck,
   Nor a cloth upon his face,
Nor drop feet foremost through the floor
   Into an empty space.

OSCAR WILDE (1856–1900)

Verses Made on the Eve of His Execution

Even such is time, which takes in trust
   Our youth, our joys, and all we have,
And pays us but with age and dust,
   Which in the dark and silent grave,
When we have wandered all our ways,
Shuts up the story of our days;
   But from this earth, this grave, this dust,
   My God shall raise me up, I trust.

SIR WALTER RALEIGH (1552–1618)

Death, Be Not Proud

Death, be not proud, though some have callèd thee
Mighty and dreadful, for thou art not so,
For those whom thou think'st thou dost overthrow,
Die not, poor Death, nor yet canst thou kill me;
From rest and sleep, which but thy pictures be,
Much pleasure, then from thee, much more must flow,
And soonest our best men with thee do go,
Rest of their bones, and soul's delivery.
Thou art slave to fate, chance, kings and desperate men,
And dost with poison, war and sickness dwell,
And poppy or charms can make us sleep as well,
And better than thy stroke; why swell'st thou then?
One short sleep past, we wake eternally,
And death shall be no more. Death, thou shalt die.

JOHN DONNE (1572–1631)

A Quoi Bon Dire

Seventeen years ago you said
Something that sounded like Goodbye;
   And everybody thinks that you are dead,
      But I.

   So I, as I grow stiff and cold,
To this and that say Goodbye too;
   And everybody sees that I am old,
      But you.

   And one fine morning in a sunny lane
Some boy and girl will meet and kiss and swear
   That nobody can love their way again,
      While over there
You will have smiled, I shall have tossed your hair.

CHARLOTTE MEW (1869–1928)

Dirge

Why were you born when the snow was falling?
You should have come to the cuckoo's calling,
Or when grapes are green in the cluster,
Or, at least, when lithe swallows muster
   For their far off flying
   From summer dying.

Why did you die when the lambs were cropping?
You should have died at the apples' dropping,
When the grasshopper comes to trouble,
And the wheatfields are sodden stubble,
   And all winds go sighing
   For sweet things dying.

CHRISTINA ROSSETTI (1830–94)

Stanzas

I'll not weep that thou art going to leave me,
    There's nothing lovely here;
And doubly will the dark world grieve me,
    While thy heart suffers there.

I'll not weep, because the summer's glory
    Must always end in gloom;
And, follow out the happiest story –
    It closes with a tomb!

And I am weary of the anguish
    Increasing winters bear;
Weary to watch the spirit languish
    Through years of dead despair.

So, if a tear, when thou art dying,
    Should haply fall from me,
It is but that my soul is sighing,
    To go and rest with thee.

EMILY BRONTË (1818–48)

A Valediction

If we must part,
Then let it be like this;
Not heart on heart,
Nor with the useless anguish of a kiss;
But touch mine hand and say:
'Until tomorrow or some other day,
If we must part.'

Words are so weak
When love hath been so strong:
Let silence speak:
'Life is a little while, and love is long;
A time to sow and reap,
And after harvest a long time to sleep,
But words are weak.'

ERNEST DOWSON (1867–1900)

Be Near Me

Be near me when my light is low,
    When the blood creeps, and the nerves prick
    And tingle; and the heart is sick,
And all the wheels of Being slow.

Be near me when the sensuous frame
    Is rack'd with pangs that conquer trust;
    And Time, a maniac scattering dust,
And Life, a Fury slinging flame.

Be near me when my faith is dry,
    And men the flies of latter spring,
    That lay their eggs, and sting and sing
And weave their petty cells and die.

Be near me when I fade away,
    To point the term of human strife,
    And on the low dark verge of life
The twilight of eternal day.

ALFRED, LORD TENNYSON (1809–92)

Beside the Bed

Someone has shut the shining eyes, straightened and
                                    folded
   The wandering hands quietly covering the unquiet
                                    breast:
So, smoothed and silenced you lie, like a child, not again
                            to be questioned or scolded:
   But, for you, not one of us believes that this is rest.

Not so to close the windows down can cloud and deaden
   The blue beyond: or to screen the wavering flame
                                    subdue its breath:
Why, if I lay my check to your cheek, your grey lips, like
                            dawn, would quiver and redden,
   Breaking into the old, odd smile at this fraud of death.

Because all night you have not turned to us or spoken
   It is time for you to wake; your dreams were never
                                    very deep:

I, for one, have seen the thin, bright, twisted threads of
　　　　　them dimmed suddenly and broken.
This is only a most piteous pretence of sleep!

CHARLOTTE MEW (1870–1928)

A Farewell

With all my will, but much against my heart,
We two now part.
My Very Dear,
Our solace is the sad road lies so clear.
It needs no art,
With faint, averted feet
And many a tear,
In our opposèd paths to persevere.
Go thou to east, I west.
We will not say
There's any hope, it is so far away.

But, O my Best,
When the one darling of our widowhead,
The nursling Grief,
Is dead,
And no dews blur our eyes
To see the peach-bloom come in evening skies,
Perchance we may,
Where now this night is day,
And even through faith of still averted feet,
Making full circle of our banishment,
Amazèd meet;
The bitter journey to the bourne so sweet
Seasoning the termless feast of our content
With tears of recognition never dry.

COVENTRY PATMORE (1823–96)

Music at My Passing

Kindly watcher by my bed, lift no voice in prayer,
Waste not any words on me when the hour is nigh,
Let a stream of melody but flow from one sweet player
And meekly will I lay my head and fold my hands to die.
    Sick I am of idle words past all reconciling,
    Words that weary and perplex and ponder and conceal:
    Wake the sounds that never lie for all their
                      sweet beguiling,
    Language one need fathom not but only hear and feel.
Let them roll once more to me and ripple in my hearing
Like waves upon a lonely beach where no one anchoreth,
That I may steep my soul in them and, craving
                      naught nor fearing,
Drift thro' slumber to a dream and thro' a dream to death.

RENÉ SULLY-PRUDHOLME (1839–1907)
adapted by GEORGE DU MAURIER (1834–96)

There's been a Death

There's been a death in the opposite house
    As lately as today.
I know it by the numb look
    Such houses have alway.

The neighbours rustle in and out,
    The doctor drives away.
A window opens like a pod,
    Abrupt, mechanically;

Somebody flings a mattress out,
    The children hurry by;
They wonder if it died on that –
    I used to when a boy.

The minister goes stiffly in
    As if the house were his
And he owned all the mourners now,
    And little boys besides;

And then the milliner, and the man
    Of the appalling trade,
To take the measure of the house.
    There'll be that dark parade

Of tassels and of coaches soon;
    It's easy as a sign –
The intuition of the news
    In just a country town.

EMILY DICKINSON (1830–86)

The Last Signal

Silently I footed by an uphill road
That led from my abode to a spot yew-boughed;
Yellowly the sun sloped low down to westward,
    And dark was the east with cloud.

Then, amid the shadow of that livid sad east,
  Where the light was least, and a gate stood wide,
Something flashed the fire of the sun that was facing it,
  Like a brief blaze on that side.

Looking hard and harder I knew what it meant –
  The sudden shine sent from the livid east scene;
It meant the west mirrored by the coffin of my
                                      friend there,
  Turning to the road from his green,

To take his last journey forth – he who in his prime
  Trudged so many a time from that gate athwart
                                      the land!
Thus a farewell to me he signalled on his grave-way,
  As with a wave of his hand.

THOMAS HARDY (1840–1928)

The Last Invocation

At the last, tenderly,
From the walls of the powerful fortressed house,
From the clasp of the knitted locks, from the
                              keep of the well-closed doors,
Let me be wafted.

Let me glide noiselessly forth;
With the key of softness unlock the locks –
                              with a whisper,
Set ope the doors O soul.

Tenderly – be not impatient
(Strong is your hold O mortal flesh.
Strong is your hold O love).

WALT WHITMAN (1819–92)

Remember

Remember me when I am gone away,
Gone far away into the silent land;
When you can no more hold me by the hand,
Nor I half turn to go, yet turning stay.
Remember me when no more, day by day.
You tell me of our future that you planned;
Only remember me; you understand
It will be late to counsel then or pray.
Yet if you should forget me for a while
And afterwards remember, do not grieve;
For if the darkness and corruption leave
A vestige of the thoughts that once I had,
Better by far you should forget and smile
Than that you should remember and be sad.

CHRISTINA ROSSETTI (1830–94)

Midnight, 30 June 1879

On the death of his brother Charles

Midnight – in no midsummer tune
   The breakers lash the shores:
The cuckoo of a joyless June
   Is calling out of doors:

And thou hast vanish'd from thine own
   To that which looks like rest,
True brother, only to be known
   By those who love thee best.

Midnight – and joyless June gone by,
   And from the deluged park
The cuckoo of a worse July
   Is calling thro' the dark:

But thou art silent underground,
   And o'er thee streams the rain,
True poet, surely to be found
   When Truth is found again.

And now to these unsummer'd skies
    The summer bird is still,
Far off a phantom cuckoo cries
    From out a phantom hill;

And thro' this midnight breaks the sun
    Of sixty years away,
The light of days when life begun,
    The days that seem today,

When all my griefs were shared with thee,
    And all my hopes were thine –
As all thou wert was one with me,
    May all thou art be mine!

ALFRED, LORD TENNYSON (1809–92)

On the Death of George Meredith

Forty years back, when much had place
That since has perished out of mind,
I heard that voice and saw that face.

He spoke as one afoot will wind
A morning horn ere men awake;
His note was trenchant, turning kind.

He was of those whose wit can shake
And riddle to the very core
The counterfeits that time will break . . .

Of late, when we two met once more,
The luminous countenance and rare
Shone just as forty years before,

So that, when now all tongues declare
His shape unseen by his green hill,
I scarce believe he sits not there.

No matter. Further and further still
Through the world's vaporous vitiate air
His words wing on – as live words will.

THOMAS HARDY (1840–1928)

Now Finale to the Shore

Now finale to the shore,
Now land and life finale and farewell,
Now voyager depart (much, much for thee is yet in store).
Often enough has thou adventured o'er the seas,
Cautiously cruising, studying the charts,
Duly again to port and hawser's tie returning;
But now obey that cherished secret wish,
Embrace thy friends, leave all in order,
To port and hawser's tie no more returning,
Depart upon thy endless cruise, old sailor!

WALT WHITMAN (1819–92)

The Old Armchair

I love it, I love it; and who shall dare
To chide me for loving that old armchair?
I've treasured it long as a sainted prize;
I've bedewed it with tears and embalmed it with sighs;
'Tis bound with a thousand bands to my heart;
Not a tie will break, not a link will start.
Would ye learn the spell? A mother sat there;
And a sacred thing is that old armchair.

In childhood's hour I lingered near
The hallowed seat with listening ear;
And gentle words that mother would give;
To fit me to die and teach me to live.
She told me shame would never betide,
With truth for my creed and God for my guide;
She taught me to lisp my earliest prayer;
As I knelt beside that old armchair.

I sat and watched her many a day,
When her eye grew dim, and her locks were grey;
And I almost worshipped her when she smiled,
And turned from her Bible to bless her child.
Years rolled on; but the last one sped:
I learned how much the heart can bear,
When I saw her die in that old armchair.

'Tis past, 'tis past, but I gaze on it now
With quivering breath and throbbing brow;
'Twas there she nursed me, 'twas there she died;
And memory flows with lava tide,
Say it is folly and deem me weak,
While the scalding drops start down my cheek;
But I love it, I love it, and cannot tear
My soul from a mother's old armchair.

ELIZA COOK (1818–89)

How Many Times These Low Feet Staggered

How many times these low feet staggered,
Only the soldered mouth can tell!
Try! can you stir the awful rivet?
Try! can you lift the hasps of steel?

Stroke the cool forehead, hot so often,
Lift, if you can, the listless hair;
Handle the adamantine fingers
Never a thimble more shall wear.

Buzz the dull flies on the chamber window;
Brave shines the sun through the freckled pane;
Fearless the cobweb swings from the ceiling –
Indolent housewife, in daisies lain!

EMILY DICKINSON (1830–86))

Requiem

Under the wide and starry sky,
Dig the grave and let me lie.
Glad did I live and gladly die,
    And I laid me down with a will.

This be the verse you grave for me:
Here he lies where he longed to be;
Home is the sailor, home from sea,
    And the hunter home from the hill.

ROBERT LOUIS STEVENSON (1850–94)

Requiescat

Tread lightly, she is near
    Under the snow,
Speak gently, she can hear
    The daisies grow.

All her bright golden hair
   Tarnished with rust,
She that was young and fair
   Fallen to dust.

Lily-like, white as snow,
   She hardly knew
She was a woman, so
   Sweetly she grew.

Coffin-board, heavy stone,
   Lie on her breast;
I vex my heart alone,
   She is at rest.

Peace, peace; she cannot hear
   Lyre or sonnet;
All my life's buried here,
   Heap earth upon it.

OSCAR WILDE (1856–1900)

A Slumber Did My Spirit Seal

A slumber did my spirit seal;
   I had no human fears:
She seemed a thing that could not feel
   The touch of earthly years.

No motion has she now, no force;
   She neither hears nor sees,
Rolled round in earth's diurnal course
   With rocks and stones and trees.

WILLIAM WORDSWORTH (1770–1850)

We Never Know We Go

We never know we go – when we are going
   We jest and shut the door;
Fate following behind us bolts it,
   And we accost no more.

EMILY DICKINSON (1830–86)

Go by, Go by

Come not, when I am dead,
   To drop thy foolish tears upon my grave,
To trample round my fallen head,
   And vex the unhappy dust thou wouldst not save.
There let the wind sweep and the plover cry;
   But thou, go by.

Child, if it were thine error or thy crime
   I care no longer, being all unblest:
Wed whom thou wilt, but I am sick of time,
   And I desire to rest.
Pass on, weak heart, and leave me where I lie;
   Go by, go by.

ALFRED, LORD TENNYSON (1809–92)

Upon the Death of Sir Albert Morton's Wife

He first deceased: she for a little tried
To live without him: liked it not, and died.

SIR HENRY WOTTON (1568–1639)

Putting Love Away

The bustle in a house
The morning after death
Is solemnest of industries
Enacted upon earth –

The sweeping up the heart
And putting love away
We shall not want to use again
Until eternity.

EMILY DICKINSON (1830–86)

Rain

Rain, midnight rain, nothing but the wild rain
On this bleak hut, and solitude, and me
Remembering again that I shall die
And neither hear the rain nor give it thanks
For washing me cleaner than I have been
Since I was born into this solitude.
Blessed are the dead that the rain rains upon:
But here I pray that none whom once I loved
Is dying tonight or lying still awake
Solitary, listening to the rain,
Either in pain or thus in sympathy
Helpless among the living and the dead,
Like a cold water among broken reeds,
Myriads of broken reeds all still and stiff,
Like me who have no love which this wild rain
Has not dissolved except the love of death,
If love it be for what is perfect and
Cannot, the tempest tells me, disappoint.

EDWARD THOMAS (1878–1917)

Crossing the Bar

Sunset and evening star,
   And one clear call for me!
And may there be no moaning of the bar,
   When I put out to sea,

But such a tide as moving seems asleep,
   Too full for sound and foam,
When that which drew from out the boundless deep
   Turns again home.

Twilight and evening bell,
   And after that the dark!
And may there be no sadness of farewell,
   When I embark;

For though from out our bourne of time and place
   The flood may bear me far,
I hope to see my Pilot face to face
   When I have crossed the bar.

ALFRED, LORD TENNYSON (1809–92)

In After Days

In after days when grasses high
O'ertop the stone where I shall lie,
 Though ill or well the world adjust
 My slender claim to honoured dust,
I shall not question or reply.

I shall not see the morning sky;
I shall not hear the night-wind's sigh;
 I shall be mute, as all men must
  In after days!

But yet, now living, fain were I
That someone then should testify,
 Saying – 'He held his pen in trust
 To art, not serving shame or lust.'
Will none? – Then let my memory die
  In after days!

HENRY AUSTIN DOBSON (1840–1921)

Dregs

The fire is out, and spent the warmth thereof
(This is the end of every song man sings!),
The golden wine is drunk, the dregs remain,
Bitter as wormwood and as salt as pain;
And health and hope have gone the way of love
Into the drear oblivion of lost things.
Ghosts go along with us until the end;
This was a mistress, this, perhaps, a friend.
With pale, indifferent eyes, we sit and wait
For the dropt curtain and the closing gate:
This is the end of all the songs man sings.

ERNEST DOWSON (1867–1900)

At the Last

And when he saw that he through all had past,
He dy'd, lest he should idle grow at last.

ABRAHAM COWLEY (1618–67)

After Death

After Death nothing is, and nothing Death;
The utmost limits of a gasp of breath.
Let the ambitious zealot lay aside
His hopes of heaven (whose faith is but his pride);
Let slavish souls lay by their fear,
Nor be concerned which way, or where,
After this life we shall be hurl'd:
Dead, we become the lumber of the world,
And to that mass of matter shall be swept
Where things destroy'd with things unborn are kept;
Devouring time swallows us whole,
Impartial Death confounds body and soul.
For hell and the foul fiend that rules
The everlasting fiery goals,
Devis'd by rogues, dreaded by fools,
With his grim grizzly dog that keeps the door,
Are senseless stories, idle tales,
Dreams, whimseys, and no more.

JOHN WILMOT, EARL OF ROCHESTER (1647–80)

A Cemetery

This quiet dust was gentlemen and ladies,
    And lads and girls;
Was laughter and ability and sighing
    And frocks and curls.
This passive place a summer's humble mansion,
    Where bloom and bees
Fulfilled their oriental circuit,
    Then ceased like these.

EMILY DICKINSON (1830–86)

In Memoriam (Easter, 1915)

The flowers left thick at nightfall in the wood
This Eastertide call into mind the men,
Now far from home, who, with their sweethearts, should
Have gathered them and will do never again.

EDWARD THOMAS (1878–1917)

One Seaside Grave

Unmindful of the roses,
Unmindful of the thorn,
A reaper tired reposes
Among the gathered corn:
So might I, till the morn!

Cold as the cold Decembers,
Past as the days that set,
While only one remembers
And all the rest forget –
But one remembers yet.

CHRISTINA ROSSETTI (1830–94)

Tranquillity

That such have died enables us
   The tranquiller to die;
That such have lived, certificate
   For immortality.

EMILY DICKINSON (1830–86)

Epitaph

Near this spot
Are deposited the remains of one
Who possessed beauty without vanity,
Strength without insolence,
Courage without ferocity,
And all the virtues of man without his vices.
This praise, which would be unmeaning flattery
If inscribed over human ashes,
Is but a just tribute to the memory of
Boatswain, a dog.

LORD BYRON (1788–1824)

Life's Trades

It's such a little thing to weep,
  So short a thing to sigh;
And yet by trades the size of these
  We men and women die.

EMILY DICKINSON (1830–86)

Grave, Where is Thy Victory?

Poor soul, the centre of my sinful earth,
Fool'd by these rebel powers that thee array,
Why dost thou pine within, and suffer dearth,
Painting thy outward walls so costly gay?
Why so large cost, having so short a lease,
Dost thou upon thy fading mansion spend?
Shall worms, inheritors of this excess,
Eat up thy charge? Is this thy body's end?
Then, soul, live thou upon thy servant's loss,
And let that pine to aggravate thy store;
Buy terms divine in selling hours of dross;
Within be fed, without be rich no more:
    So shalt thou feed on Death, that feeds on men,
    And, Death once dead, there's no more dying then.

WILLIAM SHAKESPEARE (1564–1616)

Prospero's Farewell to his Magic

Our revels now are ended. These our actors,
As I foretold you, were all spirits and
Are melted into air, into thin air:
And, like the baseless fabric of this vision,
The cloud-capp'd towers, the gorgeous palaces,
The solemn temples, the great globe itself,
Yea, all which it inherit, shall dissolve
And, like this insubstantial pageant faded,
Leave not a rack behind. We are such stuff
As dreams are made on, and our little life
Is rounded with a sleep.

WILLIAM SHAKESPEARE (1564–1616), *The Tempest*, 4, 1

Index of first lines

Creeps in half wanton, half asleep 97

Daisies are white upon the churchyard sod 72
Day breaks on England down the Kentish hills 280
Dear, back my wounded heart restore 248
Dear! of all happy in the hour, most blest 282
Death, be not proud, though some have callèd thee 362
Dispersed is all its chivalry 65
Does the road wind uphill all the way? 301
Drink to me only with thine eyes 223
Drowning is not so pitiful 326

Earth has not anything to show more fair 189
England, with all thy faults, I love thee still 179
Even such is time, which takes in trust 361

Fair daffodils, we weep to see 144
Fair summer droops, droop men and beasts therefore 150
Faith is a fine invention 336
Fall, leaves, fall; die, flowers, away 155
Farewell, farewell! but this I tell 336
Farewell! thou art too dear for my possessing 250
Faster than fairies, faster than witches 26
Fear no more the heat o' the sun 289

He did not wear his scarlet coat 358
He did the utmost bounds of knowledge find 109
He first deceased: she for a little tried 388
He gazed and gazed and gazed and gazed 17
He is starke mad, who ever sayes 251
He lived amidst th' untrodden ways 103
He or she that hopes to gain 246
He that is down needs fear no fall 319
He thought he saw an elephant 112
He was a man; take him for all in all 279
He who bends to himself a joy 202
Her name is at my tongue whene'er I speak 246
Here lies Fred 120
Here lies Our Sovereign Lord the King 113
Here malice, rapine, accident conspire 191
How do I love thee? Let me count the ways 214
How do you know that the pilgrim track 140
How happy a thing were a wedding 240
How many times these low feet staggered 383
How pleasant to know Mr Lear! 98
How sleep the brave, who sink to rest 267

I always thought a touch of blue 129

Nay, but you, who do not love her 216
Near this spot 396
Never seek to tell thy love 254
No coward soul is mine 356
'No, no; for my virginity 121
Not a drum was heard, not a funeral note 275
Not knowing when the dawn will come 342
Nothing is so beautiful as spring 142
Now, even, I cannot think it true 346
Now finale to the shore 380
Now sleeps the crimson petal, now the white 220
Now winter nights enlarge 243

O fret not after knowledge – I have none 309
O more than mortall man, that did this towne begin! 190
O my luve's like a red, red rose 222
O Rose, thou art sick! 161
O that 'twere possible 60
O world invisible, we view thee 302
Oh, never weep for love that's dead 256
Oh, the wild joy of living: the leaping from rock to rock 31
Oh, to be in England 177
Oh! hear a pensive captive's prayer 134

Surprised by joy – impatient as the wind 350
Sweet day, so cool, so calm, so bright 305

Tall nettles cover up, as they have done 188
Tears, idle tears, I know not what they mean 56
Tell me not, sweet, I am unkind 268
That such have died enables us 395
That time of year thou mayst in me behold 157
The Assyrian came down like the wolf on the fold 271
The bustle in a house 388
The cherry trees bend over and are shedding 290
'The child is father to the man' 101
The earth was green, the sky was blue 146
The fire is out, and spent the warmth thereof 392
The flowers left thick at nightfall in the wood 394
The frog, half fearful, jumps across the path 151
The kingdoms of the earth go by 47
The lark now leaves his watery nest 171
The lowest trees have tops, the ant her gall 137
The mountain sheep are sweeter 269
The naked earth is warm with spring 285
The night has a thousand eyes 266
The night is darkening round me 343